The Golden Prayer Puzzle

Other Works by the Same Author

Books

Numberland
Bird
Quiet Answers
Three Gifts: The Eras of Science, Medicine, Religion

Musical plays

Numberland
Musicland

Music and dialogue recordings

Numberland
Numberland Music
Musicland
Children's Musicland
Something Bright and Beautiful
Bird
Lessons from Bird

The Golden Prayer Puzzle

By

Auriel Wyndham Livezey

Mountaintop Publishing

Copyright © 2016 Mountaintop Publishing
All rights reserved.
No part of this book may be reproduced or transmitted in any form or by any means without permission from the publisher.

Printed in the United States of America
ISBN 978-1-893930-09-4

Mountaintop Publishing
www.MountaintopPublishing.com

Contents

Introduction 9

A Golden Purpose 17

Guidebook Information 35

The Baseball Lesson 83

Golden Road Rules 103

Orientation Tour 123

All Aboard! 141

NOTE

The books of the Bible are not usually abbreviated. The works of Mary Baker Eddy are abbreviated. *Science and Health with Key to the Scriptures* will often be referred to as S&H followed by the page number.
Miscellaneous Writings is shown as Mis.
First Church of Christ, Scientist and Miscellany is My.
Retrospection and Introspection is Ret.
Rudimental Divine Science is Rud.
Message to The Mother Church for 1901 becomes Mess. '01.

THE PRAYER PATH

The path of progress
is
paved with prayer

If your path in life seems long and hard,
Not one you would have taken,
If a stumbling block is in your way
And by friends you feel forsaken,

Then face that unyielding block of stone,
Pray till it's flat and wide,
You'll find you have a stepping stone
With angels by your side.

THE GOLDEN PRAYER PUZZLE

Introduction

A most interesting statistic surfaced in the news just the other day. It was revealed that, although religion is declining with church memberships dropping, prayer is actually on the rise. Yes, the number of people who pray has increased. There was no reason given for this. After all, it was simply a statistic. One could draw their own conclusions. Perhaps these stirring times have prompted the pursuit of prayer. We can almost imagine a large stream of humanity parading down a well-known boulevard with individuals from the sidelines suddenly joining in, as though they had heard the silent music of the march.

Of course, prayer is a wide-open field that has always been accessible to humanity, needing no special membership card to enjoy its privileges or to enter its domain.

Prayer, especially silent prayer, can take place anywhere and in any situation. It could even be said that prayer is in session all around the world, all the time. It's a constant. We might even think of it in the following terms.

There is one traveler who needs no passport or visa, but freely passes through all borders and checkpoints without ever being asked for identification. You will never hear of this traveler's need for money, or for a reservation, but strange as it may sound, rarely a flight takes off without this frequent flyer no matter how fully booked it is. An invitation is never needed to any event, be it a Wimbledon tennis match, a wedding, the crowning of a monarch or the memorial service of the lowliest of citizens. The traveler is able to appear all over the world and be simultaneously present in countless places and predicaments. Furthermore, outer space is not too far, no ocean is too deep, no foxhole too dangerous for this intrepid one. Prayer is that traveler.

Now, because it travels, prayer takes us somewhere, from point A to point B. Sincere, honest, humble prayer never leaves us in the same place that it found us. Because so many have found this to be true, we won't quibble over that statement, but just accept it and go on to exploring the subject.

If we were to put prayer under a mental microscope, we would find that at the basis of prayer is a desire. It might be for something such as world peace, touted humorously in the movie *Miss Congeniality*

INTRODUCTION

as the usual answer given by contestants in a beauty pageant. Yes, one's desire may be truly altruistic or else totally unworthy, just a selfish aim. On the other hand, an infant intuitively reaches out to its parents. To be cared for and loved is a basic desire, which begins immediately when one enters the human scene. How we proceed from that point on with our desires determines not only the happiness and success of our own lives, but our contribution to the world in general.

A woman I once knew was convinced she had been wronged at her previous place of employment, not given enough credit, and wanted to sue that company. Over her family's and friends' objections to this line of action, she held on to that desire with great determination. It almost consumed her. One day, I asked how it would benefit everyone if she were to carry out her plan. What good would it add to the world? That simple question immediately removed her revengeful desire as another better one—her natural inclination to be a blessing to the world—took over. Family and friends thought it a miracle that she could change overnight, but she did!

It is apparent that our desires, our prayers, are not confined to church or religious participation. But to whom do we usually take our desires? Taking them to people is risky business. That scenario depends on another's ability or willingness to concede to our requests. On the other hand, taking our desires to God in prayer should mean submitting our plans for divine approval. In this case, a "no" answer could be just what we need. Humble prayer means we subordinate our own human will to the divine will, to the intelligence, the divine Love, we name God. Obviously, we don't always know what is best for us or mankind, but prayer and divine Love will reveal it to us.

One thing we can usually all agree upon immediately is that we yearn for the prayer that brings results—one that heals and that makes clear the answers we need. Such prayer would be considered priceless, and could be classified as golden. In other words, we would like to find the gold which is at the heart of prayer.

In this book, we'll be going on a thought expedition, because there are mysteries to be solved, which should answer many important questions. What better guide could we have than the Bible with its vivid and often graphic illustrations of the life paths to take and the ones to be avoided!

Perhaps, we could structure our expedition by the use of allegories and parables. After all, the Bible contains many such teaching tools. We learn a large lesson when reading of Jonah's disobedience being turned into obedience, after he was swallowed up in a dark experience typified by a whale's belly.

Today, many well-known Bible scholars acknowledge that some of these accounts serve as illustrations for daily living rather than being literal happenings. Jesus employed many parables

INTRODUCTION

for teaching spiritual lessons. We're all familiar, whether religious or not, with the story of the prodigal son.

Modern-day parables abound, even by e-mails, telling heart-warming, short stories that make a case for unselfishness or the need for non-judgmental attitudes. They appear to be true stories, but they can be found under the heading, on the Internet, of modern parables. Though not factual, they do carry a helpful and uplifting message for mankind.

Now, this book is multi-faceted in our quest for spiritual treasure. It's a metaphysical mystery, a scientific exploration and a spiritual search all rolled into one. In the same vein as John Bunyan's classic Christian allegory, *The Pilgrim's Progress*, we will not only begin our journey with an allegory, but parables, metaphors, and analogies will be liberally sprinkled throughout.

So, let's begin with a question. What would you think if you were given a jigsaw puzzle to piece together, while being told the clues in the puzzle would help solve perplexing questions about life, plus mysteries in the Bible, and put you on the path to search for and find the gold of prayer?

Even those who are not religiously or spiritually minded should be intrigued by at least one of those three possibilities. Besides, we all love a puzzle, a mystery of one kind or another.

For this search, we could go on a plane ride, as gaining some altitude would be an advantage. But, rather than enjoying a peaceful excursion, we'll invite our passengers to jump out of the plane instead. That isn't as strange as it sounds, is it! Extreme sports such as swimming with sharks, jumping off cliffs, or out of airplanes, were inconceivable not so long ago. Times have certainly changed!

For instance, skydiving is quite popular today. There was an account posted, a couple of years ago, on YouTube of an 82 year old woman in England, who is an avid skydiver. Then, there's the well-known training center in Perris, California, which attracts those who simply want to take part in a new sport, as well as military personnel, who are in training. Skydiving teams from Canada, and as far away as Australia, come to Perris.

In fact, an Australian team set a new National Australian record for formation skydiving with 119 people in 2015. They had trained for years to accomplish that feat. It's an inspiring account of success against all odds and is worth reading.

As a side note here, if you're simply going for a joyride, you'll take it strapped to an experienced diver in what is called tandem diving. But if you aim to learn the art of skydiving, there is a different process to go through.

At Perris, there are many avenues to assist the learner, such as a wind tunnel to acclimate one. You need to be prepared for AFF, Accelerated Free Fall. Even when the time comes for flight, you are not alone, as the jump is taken with two instructors.

More training and many more flights will take place before your first solo dive. Understandably, preparation is a huge part of this process. The right spirit is also crucial, for a lazy or devil-may-care attitude could land one in a heap of trouble, as the saying goes.

We'll explore this subject further with an allegorical tale about an intrepid skydiver and his less than stellar companions.

You'll notice that each skydiver is looking at life through his own perspective, his own filter, as do most people. The filter could be one's human expertise, preferences, or ambition, for instance

When considering subjects of such magnitude as we will be doing in this book, it's helpful to remove those filters, if at all possible. It's the "poor in spirit" and the "pure in heart" (those without the filters) who will be benefited or blessed the most by any endeavor, be it human or divine.

And now, here is where we pull back on the throttle, take off, and prepare for the skydivers—all those interested in this spiritual exploration—to jump out of their comfort zone and begin a journey of some life-changing proportion. Whether that is an overstatement or not will be up to you to determine, but only after the expedition.

In fact, friends have asked me why I am writing this book. I hope by the time you reach the end, you will know the answer.

A GOLDEN PURPOSE

A bulletin was posted at the local skydiving school stating that members, wishing for advanced credentials, should meet with an experienced skydiver for information regarding a skydiving treasure hunt. This was described as an enrichment exercise, which caused many to assume they would gather more skydiving tips from a veteran diver.

Accordingly, a good number of people signed up including a group of five business associates. These men approached the woman behind the counter and asked for information. To their surprise, this very experienced skydiver was over eighty years old. She said the flight school wanted to be sure that they were encouraging personal development as they trained their divers. A skydiver who was unaware of the finer things in life could be a liability, rather than an asset, and would definitely not be a good advertisement for the school.

She explained that there was more to life than the joy of skydiving, and that such pleasures could actually be turned into learning experiences. She, herself, had received some of her most memorable life lessons while in free fall.

The treasure hunt was aimed at helping skydivers look for joys, or ideas, of a more spiritual nature, which in turn could change their lives and help others too. One option was to sign up for that general search, and most people had.

However, there was another option. They could choose the specific assignment, which was to solve the golden prayer puzzle. That endeavor entailed seeking out invaluable items, such as hope that shines like a diamond, the gold of prayer and pearls of wisdom, but not necessarily in that order.

Which would they sign up for? That was the question. The five men, liking a challenge, decided they would solve the puzzle. Then came the details.

All skydivers would be flown to a small town, set in the middle of a rural area, about ten minutes from the skydiving school. It was there they would jump out to explore for their life-enrichment clues. At certain times, planes would pick up the seekers at the little airstrip outside of town.

The five men were given identical jigsaw puzzles, with a picture of the town, and told they needed to gain an overview by studying the cover. Putting the puzzle pieces together would show some clues and might even reveal the best jumping-off point. But, the divers were given no set structure or order for their search, or even a hint as to where to land. They had to reason it out for themselves. Finally, planes were running regularly, taking other people too, so they could leave when ready.

Work on the puzzle should begin immediately the woman told them, as she ushered them into a small room. Her final words to them were, "Remember, the best things in life are free."

The five men sat in silence for a few minutes, staring at their puzzles, and then they began to work on assembling the pieces. Suddenly, one man said he never really did care much for details. That was very true. In fact, details made Gerald Generic rather uncomfortable. When pressed for specifics on subjects, even ones important to him, he evaded the question. He might be shown up or seen as lacking, so he much preferred general statements and concepts. He remarked to his fellow skydivers that there was actually only one picture that mattered—the big picture. He would concentrate on that and not worry about putting the puzzle together.

Another skydiver took issue with Gerald's remarks. Spencer Specific pointed to the jigsaw pieces, scattered all over his table, which he was quickly forming into small cameo pictures. He had partial scenes of a park, a road, a bank, a library, a chapel and even a river. However, nothing was connected because he wasn't looking at the big picture. That's why he declared there was not one picture but many pictures. A heated discussion ensued.

Gerald Generic stuck to his position of there being only one picture, as he studied the cover of the box. Rather than taking valuable time assembling his puzzle, he decided to take off right away. He left feeling rather sorry he hadn't signed up for the general enrichment search.

Gerald boarded the plane trusting that the jump would land him where he needed to go. With his love of grand sweeping views, he soon forgot about his purpose, his golden opportunity, and simply became a sightseer. While drifting to earth in that euphoric state, he spoke aloud his joyful observations and neglected to aim at anything specifically. Not too surprisingly, Gerald ended up being tangled in a tree.

Spencer Specific smiled at the news about Gerald, as he kept perusing the pieces and shifting them around. He hardly noticed the picture on the box.

Oh, yes, Spencer was a man who loved details so much he'd even taken his red pen to mark up the instruction booklet when learning to skydive. Pointing out typos and grammatical errors made him feel so productive. He was certain his suggestions for writing a clearer flying manual would gain attention, but so far Spencer had received no accolades for his efforts.

Nevertheless, he was intent on details again. But without the help of the big picture, his puzzle wasn't coming together. Moreover, he certainly couldn't locate any specific gems in it, such as pearls, diamonds or gold. How puzzling! Spencer took so long trying to figure it all out that the last flight was being announced. He wasn't sure if he should go, or go home and try again another time. He knew he just had to study harder.

The third man heard the description of precious gems and thought he would zero in on the search for gold and prayer, as they appeared to be linked together. It was obvious he had mistaken "golden prayer puzzle" for "gold *and* prayer puzzle." Persuaded that this was a profitable venture for him and his organization—one that might finally bring him the life of leisure he desired and secure his place among the rich and famous—he scoured the puzzle for clues. The idea that prayer could be golden, and its worth applied to the needs of others, never occurred to him, for his own needs took center stage. His name was Selby Selfish.

Now, Selby did take note of some details— the most pertinent ones he thought. Taking a magnifying glass to the cover of the box, he found the town's savings bank (he could just make out the words on the building) and it was only a block or two away from a small church or chapel at the river's edge. That information was enough for him to know, as either one might contain the gold linked with prayer.

As the plane circled, Selby vacillated between landing near the chapel or the bank. His focus was "double-minded" and that meant he was unstable.

As he jumped with those motives, he lost the ability to follow procedure, to maneuver in flight or even to land properly. Selby was losing what he'd learned.

The instructors in the aircraft flying overhead noticed this, as a kind passerby helped fish Selby out of the river on his third try. It was decided that Selby would need to be certified again for solo diving, and his flying time would be given to another more deserving seeker. "I certainly tried hard enough," Selby told himself, as he gave up the search and went home to dry off.

The fourth skydiver had taken a quick look at the puzzle's picture and noted a few details, such as the town library, and commented to himself that he already had his own big picture and all the pieces he needed to reach the finer things in life. He had borrowed ideas from many scholars on the subject, especially on prayer, and put them together. His were trusted sources, well-known people, and so he felt that with their fine experience and help, he would certainly know what to do. Besides, his accumulated knowledge was so valuable, it surely would constitute the gold of prayer, or so he surmised.

Colin Collector didn't have the correct big picture in mind, but just thought he did. With confidence, he decided to aim for the library on the outskirts of town, figuring a further clue or treasure map might be hidden in one of the books there.

However, Colin was so busy mentally reviewing the many opinions he had read on prayer that he didn't notice, as he stepped out, that the plane had overshot the town. Instead of landing near the library, he ended up in a distant cow pasture. Dirty and dusty, Colin had to hitchhike back into town on the back of a truck, which he shared with a variety of farm animals. Feeling very confused, he went off to consult more sources on the subject of prayer before attempting to skydive again.

The fifth skydiver was intent from the very beginning. Because he was extremely earnest and eager, he had to watch carefully not to get carried away by the excitement of the adventure. Earnest Eager so loved the idea of a spiritual quest, of finding pearls of wisdom or golden prayer, that he decided to skydive as many times as needed. He was already filled with hope, but he was not sure it shined like a diamond, so he would be alert to watch for it also. You could say, he truly possessed the right spirit.

Earnest prepared by first studying the picture on the puzzle box, and then he took note of the details. He'd heard the quarrel between Mr. Generic and Mr. Specific, but recognized both views were important. Finally, he worked hard and thoroughly to put the pieces together. This made him very aware of the territory. For instance, in the middle of the puzzle lay a planned town center with a highway running through it up towards the river. He could tell there were spurs or detours off that highway and forks in the river, so a traveler would need to pay attention and not be misled on their journey.

This skydiver marveled at the beauty of the flowers and trees planted along the highway. He also noticed a library at one end of the town, and close to it a tiny kiosk. At the other end of town was a very small church or chapel beside the river. The highway ran up to that spot. However, nothing really stood out to him as the perfect landing place. That little church seemed a logical place to search for the gold of prayer, but Earnest hung back.

Then he remembered a conversation from one of his favorite books, *The Pilgrim's Progress.* The main character, Christian, had asked another character named Hopeful, who had been quite persistent in his search, just how the Father had shown him the Son, and this was Hopeful's reply. "I did not see him with my bodily eyes, but the eyes of mine understanding."

Earnest finally realized what he must do. He was not to look for physical signs. Intuitively, he felt the need to really understand his journey, and to do that he would first have to find the pearls of wisdom.

With that important conclusion, something came back to him. The tiny kiosk was a type of information booth for the Guidebook. Though he already had some familiarity with that book, Earnest knew it was where he needed to begin. He hoped to steer his parachute to that exact spot. With joy, Earnest sang a little song as he prepared to jump.

* * * * * * * * * * * * * *

The right spirit

Yes, Earnest Eager was well equipped with the right spirit. The others in the allegory were somehow lacking, which was obvious with our gold-seeking friend Selby Selfish, who wanted the gold for all the wrong reasons. The gold of prayer was designed to make one rich in good deeds and character, not to fatten up a bank account or an organization. In a sense, he buried his talent in the ground or, in this case, the river. As Jesus' parable foretold, the opportunity was taken from him and given to another more deserving.

Poor Colin Collector didn't possess enough of the spirit of adventure. He didn't trust his own exploration and exchanged the picture on the box with another one formed by many human opinions on the subject. He finally realized that a variety of opinions, though well intended, can land one in unfamiliar territory with strange companions.

On the surface, Mr. Generic had the right spirit, having made wonderful statements about the scenery, as he floated to earth. But his spirit was lacking in appreciation for the details of the search, an integral part of the big picture, which is why he ended up in a tree.

Mr. Specific was likewise only half-hearted, for he couldn't appreciate or value the big picture. He was all consumed by the details and instructions of the flight. Considering himself proficient in the specifics, he attempted to aid others with his expertise. He was even willing to give up the skydiving adventure in exchange for simply studying about it.

Of course, Mr. Generic and Mr. Specific were both right and wrong, for their views weren't complete without each other, nor could they really solve anything without both perspectives.

Earnest Eager had the joy of the journey and search. His was not a begrudging effort but an animated obedience. We all know it's not simply what we do, but the spirit in which we do it that counts. There are enthusiasm, joy and brotherly love to be shared, or else how can we claim to be animated by the divine Spirit, God.

That brings us to the story of a woman who tended to be enthusiastic to the point where she sometimes would overwhelm her audience. A friend once told her "your enthusiasm sweeps over me like a tsunami!" So, she decided to curb any overabundance of that commodity and was diligent at a board meeting she attended. Rather quietly, she suggested a course of action, at which another board member immediately exclaimed, "Stay calm! Stay calm!" The woman said if she'd been any calmer she would have been flat on the floor! This might make us wonder if, in this politically-correct period, animation is more appreciated on the big screen. For instance, the animated film *Finding Dory* might be more popular than the real-life picture of enthusiastic seekers finding the gold of prayer. Animated people, motivated in a good direction, could even be viewed with suspicion or envy.

The problem isn't new. Cain and Abel in the book of Genesis were faced with a similar situation. Cain's means of living was the fruit of the ground, while Abel's was in sheep. So, when each made an offering to the Lord from their resources, Cain's was quite different from Abel's, whose offering was more acceptable to God. *Science and Health with Key to the Scriptures* by Mary Baker Eddy explains it this way on page 540: "A lamb is a more animate form of existence, and more nearly resembles a mind-offering than does Cain's fruit."

Surely, it would not be inaccurate to assume that Cain was "cool as a cucumber," and not possessing the same spirit as animated Abel. How important the right spirit is to any endeavor or exploration! However, it all needs to be kept in balance, which is often no small task. The operative word here might be temperance. Sometimes enthusiasm, and lack of an overview, could even be dangerous as evidenced by the following.

The importance of generic and specific

A man I knew was a worldwide authority on birds, including flightless birds, and he would explore different regions as part of the grants he gained for research. He was an avid, enthusiastic and excellent researcher.

This is where the importance of having both generic and specific views enters the story. Our researcher had traveled to the Falkland Islands and chosen a spot where he could lie down in the tall grass to observe the birds in that area of the world. With his powerful binoculars trained on the birds, he lay there undetected—or so he thought. The close-up or specific view would testify to a peaceful process—a man quietly lying in the grass with binoculars.

However, zoom out a little on the distance, and you will notice a military installation not far from the birds in question. Then zoom out on the figure in the grass, and you will further note a teenage boy, a little distance behind the birdwatcher, with a rifle trained at his head.

Yes, the big picture was anything but peaceful and for one good reason. During that period, the Falklands were at war! And engaged in that fracas were both British and American troops. Happily, our American friend was able to extricate himself from that situation.

Our birdwatcher's enthusiasm, and his concentration on the details of the quest, made him blind to the big picture. The effect of this loss, in a religious context, is explained in a statement by Mary Baker Eddy.

> Losing the comprehensive in the technical, the Principle in its accessories, cause in effect, and

faith in sight, we lose the Science of Christianity, — a predicament quite like that of the man who could not see London for its houses. (My. 149)

Now, Gerald Generic might smile knowingly at that predicament, for he didn't care to concentrate on details. He was all about the big picture. Yes, he might have even doled out an "I told you so" to the birdwatcher.

Of course, details are important, but not simply in themselves, or for their own sake, as Spencer Specific would have them, but as an expression of a larger fact. We can't progress or achieve great heights in any endeavor without specifics. This was even true of Christ Jesus, and Mrs. Eddy explained how the Christ, or incorporeal idea of Truth, specifically entered the life of the Master.

> This spiritual idea, or Christ, entered into the minutiae of the life of the personal Jesus. It made him an honest man, a good carpenter, and a good man, before it could make him the glorified. (Mis. 166)

By concentrating on only one or the other, the generic or specific, we would actually form a two-sided object about which to argue rather than seeing one cohesive picture.

This is somewhat similar to the legend of the shield, mentioned in *Science and Health*, where two knights quarreled because each could see only one side of it, and both sides were different.

Competing views, and therefore competition, can unwittingly take place even among friends. A woman remarked she had begun to work at sixteen, to which her friend immediately replied, "I started at fourteen." But, the first worked full-time at sixteen, and the other began to babysit at fourteen. Details do make a difference!

Honest details are being demanded of political candidates, who make sweeping statements about their proposals, or even their own private lives, without specifics to back it all up. This scientific era demands specificity, otherwise there is no accurate picture. And the specifics without the overall view would be meaningless.

Now, you may wonder at this point why so much is being made of these concepts. After all, it appears we are just making fine linguistic distinctions that appear infrequently by name in *Science and Health* and not at all in the Bible. That's true, but this construction is often used, if not named, to express spiritual facts, and therefore it is of great importance. It's necessary to acquaint ourselves with the idea, for the subject is not usually discussed, and yet it holds the key to solving perplexing Biblical questions and metaphysical teachings, as well as everyday problems.

A GOLDEN PURPOSE

So, I'll ask for your patience as we explore this dimension of understanding. We'll need to look at it from a number of angles and situations to really get around the subject, as it seems almost too mundane, too commonplace, to possess a great deal of significance, and yet it is a problem solver of major proportion.

Furthermore, our moral and spiritual progress requires this clarity, and our human relationships demand it. All the rightly-balanced enthusiasm, or true spirit we can muster, will not compensate for the lack of understanding both generic and specific explanations in any department of life.

Mistaken verbiage, to do with generic and specific, can easily lead to altercations in the business world, in national affairs, among religions, and even between those of the same religion. From small irritations to a rift or even large chasm, one can often find the culprit hiding behind these two innocent looking, inseparable concepts. Specific naturally follows generic, and generic can't stand on its own without the specific, but confuse the two, and one could land in a troublesome situation. Let's just take one small instance of that in business.

A successful man was reporting to the Board of Directors of his company. His references to "you can't really do that," or "you've got to know," were challenged by an irate Board member, who told the man not to tell him what to do. Another Board member immediately spoke up with, "He's not talking specifically about you, Ted, or about any of us. He's just talking in general."

In society, or in a social setting, the confusion between a generic or specific situation could inadvertently produce lack of compassion for another's plight. That was apparent when two women visited a new kitchen in a business establishment. One woman remarked that the workers were eating their lunch standing at the kitchen sink. The other woman replied that she usually ate lunch standing at her kitchen sink. Both general statements were correct, but the specifics were totally different. In one case, the kitchen workers had no table and no option to sit down, whereas the woman, with a well-appointed home, chose to stand at the sink.

Now, what about the thinkers of the world? Are they impacted by the concept of generic and specific? Let's look at groupthink. The common concept of "groupthink" is explained in Wikipedia as a group taking a course of action without viewing any dissenting opinions or gaining enlightenment on the subject. Immediately after that description is the posting of a Patrick Tay in Singapore, who heads his column, "The Fallacy of Groupthink." His writing points out that there is usually a dominant individual within the group, and that person has influenced the actions of the others.

So, is groupthink really thinking by a group or merely an individual's strong influence? Well, we could say, in most cases, it is probably both. One is a general overview of the group and is correct. Groupthink is taking place. On closer inspection, there often is a strong individual's influence at work. It's another instance of generic and specific confusion, and the ensuing disagreement over the two. Gerald Generic would agree with Wikipedia, while Spencer Specific would side with Patrick Tay.

Generic and specific differences can also be a matter of time. If the contrast of the generic to the specific is out of time, that would be an anachronism. A painting that depicts a knight in armor wearing a wrist watch would be an example, for wrist watches didn't exist then. The detail is wrong for that period.

There have even been surprising reports of soldiers hiding out for years on the islands and in the jungles of the South Pacific, totally unaware that the big picture had changed. The war was over!

Another example of that is being enacted right now as churches try to carry on in the usual manner, or with some variation on the theme, while not recognizing that the era has changed. It is now a scientific era in the United States, for instance, not a religious one. First, it will require an honest look at that big picture, the new era, and all it entails. Then it will take some adapting or evolving for the religious element to contribute meaningfully to this period. If they don't, they will at some point also constitute an anachronism.

Let us consider one last example of generic and specific terms from the field of religion, for it was actually through this experience that I found it possible to be generically correct and specifically wrong. An argument was the seed that sprang up and blossomed for me sometime later.

A student of Christian Science related how puzzled she was by a conversation between two very seasoned students. She said they argued as to whether there was only one man or many men.

That question lingered in my thinking for some time. In reasoning it out, it became obvious that they were both correct, but one was talking generically and the other specifically. There is, generically and spiritually speaking, only one kind of man, therefore one man, who is the spiritual idea of the one God. This man is a compound idea.

But the close-up, specific view shows a multitude of both men and women under that heading of man. *Science and Health* covers this in one succinct statement on page 267, "Generically man is one, and specifically man means all men."

So, my question was answered, but it didn't stop there. It also provided an important insight for further discovery.

Now, it may surprise you, as it did me, to find that the understanding of generic and specific helps to solve some of our largest Biblical questions.

That sounds like a grandiose statement, doesn't it! Well, we can stop by the Guidebook information kiosk and find out.

GUIDEBOOK INFORMATION

Earnest Eager landed well and neatly packed up his parachute, happy that he had achieved his goal to land near the little kiosk that contained the Guidebook information.

There were a couple of skydivers from the flight school there already, and they seemed to be arguing with the attendant. After a minute or two, they left without any apparent satisfaction, which Earnest deduced from their departing comments. Not wanting to disturb the attendant any further, he approached her in a quiet manner and asked what he could learn about gaining wisdom and understanding at the kiosk.

The attendant, appearing quite calm and unruffled, inquired as to what he had learned that very morning. Earnest told her about his skydiving companions, especially Gerald Generic and Spencer Specific and their argument. The attendant was surprised and obviously intrigued by his answer. Opening the Guidebook, she began showing Earnest different places where he could apply the understanding he had already gained. Earnest was quite amazed.

She further explained how important it was to approach the Guidebook humbly without any false enthusiasm, so the traveler would not simply be following it on blind faith. That could lead one astray, up blind alleys, and into a state of confusion where hopelessness reigned.

That statement made Earnest shudder, so he inquired if it would be difficult to really understand the book. He so yearned for true understanding, not blind faith, and certainly not false enthusiasm.

The attendant smiled and told him very gently that the pearls of wisdom found in the book were valuable beyond compare and were completely genuine. They would anchor him. Then she handed him another book, which she referred to as the Key book, to unlock the mysteries of the Guidebook.

The final words of the attendant were, "Don't begin your journey until you visit the baseball shop a few doors down from here. That is, after you've gone over what we discussed." That seemed rather strange to Earnest, but he figured it had to be a clue. On leaving, he settled down on a nearby bench to examine his books and contemplate the perplexing questions in the Guidebook. He was grateful for Gerald and Spencer, because their disagreement actually held a very large clue to the mysteries. It was like pulling on a string and having all the hard-to-understand sayings unravel one after another.

* * * * * * * * * * * * * * *

The Guidebook and a book with a Key

The Guidebook, to which we all have access, is the Bible, which depicts the truth of life, and the error of our beliefs about life. Then it takes us on a journey to reach reality and the truth of our being.

Why is the Bible the Guidebook for countless thousands—students of Christian Science among them? The first tenet of Christian Science may just answer that for many seekers. "As adherents of Truth we take the inspired Word of the Bible as our sufficient guide to eternal life." (S&H 496)

Actually, the Bible is like an ancient treasure map that shows paths by parables, contains puzzling statements and mysteries to be solved. Efforts to decipher it have continued throughout the ages, and so the countless diverse opinions about the book's contents have clouded the practical truths. *Science and Health with Key to the Scriptures* by Mary Baker Eddy removes the cloud and reveals that the Bible is totally practical.

Opinions abound on every level and on every subject, it seems. The human scene is so populated with them, that they go almost unnoticed. For instance, it's almost impossible to read or hear a news report without the speculation given as to the whys and wherefores of a situation. (*The Christian Science Monitor* has a reputation for avoiding the speculation pitfall in its reporting.) Let's explore this subject for a moment.

Zeal and details

This lesson regarding human opinions took place, when my husband Glen and I lived on top of Palomar Mountain in Southern California from 1982 to 1985. We had purchased a small, picturesque house that was situated in the middle of ten beautiful, wooded acres. The house required some repairs and renovation, while the property itself needed to be dispossessed of thirty years' accumulation of various items. It took half of our time there to finally clear the land of such oddities as an I-beam, huge water tank, buggy, antique cars, and ships' paraphernalia. (The former owner had been a seafaring man.)

Perhaps, you can imagine that much physical labor on the property accompanied the life lessons we were learning. Yes, we considered that tiny residence to be our classroom for spiritual lessons.

One of the lessons took place over the span of about two weeks. We called it our "not surmising, or not speculating" period. It became very obvious that even a simple message of someone's leaving town could cause us to conjecture as to the reasons why. In other words, we filled in the details with our opinions, and they were invariably wrong. In fact, they were so consistently wrong, we'd jokingly say to each other, "wrong again." From this, we learned to ask for specifics of what we were being told, if it seemed important enough to know, rather than merely speculate.

Society appears to have a Gerald Generic view of events, and constantly fills in its own details without troubling to search for the truth of the situation. This tendency could render one either hopeless or exceedingly and falsely hopeful. The latter might appear joyful, but is actually quite harmful.

The Bible warns of that very attitude through our friend Paul. Formerly, as Saul, he was particularly zealous in persecuting Christians, though he had no knowledge of what they were truly about. When he did understand, through his conversion to Paul, he gave the Romans (10:1-3) a strong warning about zeal without knowledge.

> Brethren, my heart's desire and prayer to God for Israel is, that they might be saved.
>
> For I bear them record that they have a zeal of God, but not according to knowledge.
>
> For they being ignorant of God's righteousness, and going about to establish their own righteousness, have not submitted themselves unto the righteousness of God.

Mary Baker Eddy likewise gave two distinct warnings, and one was about prayer. She preferred silent prayer, for it expressed more genuinely one's honest desire. Of audible prayer she stated:

> Looking deeply into these things, we find that "a zeal . . .not according to knowledge" gives occasion for reaction unfavorable to spiritual growth, sober resolve, and wholesome perception of God's requirements. (S&H 7)

She also warns of this extreme human emotion when involved in our work with Christian Science.

> Even the humanitarian at work in this field of limitless power and good may possess a zeal without knowledge, and thus mistake the sphere of his present usefulness. (Mis. 284)

The emotional fervor and frenzy sometimes evidenced by those in religion is more than off-putting to those who prefer to be enlightened through reason, prayer and revelation. In other words, through spiritual understanding rather than blind belief.

Filling in the details is particularly dangerous when we're dealing with spiritual truths. The honest question to be asked of ourselves is: How much of what I believe is simply my, or someone else's, opinion?

In fact, how much of religion today contains details that have simply been filled in and provided by human opinions?

Now, on the other side of this is a true or genuine enthusiasm for all that is good. The joy of imparting anything worthwhile can be found under the first part of the definition of zeal in *Science and Health*. Both sides, you'll notice, are in this definition, as the true and the false sense are described.

> ZEAL. The reflected animation of Life, Truth, and Love. Blind enthusiasm; mortal will. (S&H 598)

And Mrs. Eddy also wrote: "Do not forget that an honest, wise zeal, a lowly, triumphant trust, a true heart, and a helping hand constitute man, and nothing less is man or woman." (My. 259)

The zeal that is "the reflected animation of Life, Truth, and Love" has a firm bedrock of understanding. Zeal without knowledge puts one at risk on shaky ground. The beginning of this book dealt with having the right spirit. A venture that is not undertaken with that spirit will be undermined to the point of failure. How necessary it is to allow for and cultivate the joy of right enthusiasm!

Aiming for the true idea of animation, rather than the false, will also move us out of any halfway point of wishy-washy, bland, unenergized work for God. We need to take off the kid gloves!

Mrs. Eddy put this as probing questions, topped off with a rousing imperative.

> Will you doff your lavender-kid zeal, and become real and consecrated warriors? Will you give yourselves wholly and irrevocably to the great work of establishing the truth, the gospel, and the Science which are necessary to the salvation of the world from error, sin, disease, and death? Answer at once and practically, and answer aright! (Mis. 177)

Now, I've digressed a little by filling in more specifics from the books on the subject of zeal, and yet in a way this is right on target.

Under the heading "Admonition," the Discoverer of Christian Science encouraged us.

> Be temperate in thought, word, and deed. Meekness and temperance are the jewels of Love, set in wisdom. Restrain untempered zeal. (Ret.79)

We were talking about how religion has filled in the details of the Bible's teaching with its own speculation. Then, there's just general opinion doing the same thing. Oh, this was all well intended, no doubt about that, but the intentions don't necessarily render the details correct, and now we'll begin to explore why that is.

No guilt trip

Earnest Eager may have to curb any false zeal as he starts out on his important journey, but he is not being sent out on a guilt trip, and neither are we!

It's strange that even those who aren't doing anything wrong specifically can often still entertain a general uneasiness, a subtle feeling of guilt.

A policeman once publicly admitted that when off-duty, driving his own car, he felt apprehensive whenever a police car approached or passed him.

Why is this? Why would perfectly innocent people, including those who work for law and order, feel intimidated coming into close contact with the law? We all know that feeling, and how we attempt to act nonchalantly, when a police car draws abreast of us at a stop light. It's as though we're trying to convey the message, "Hey, see how relaxed I am? That's because I'm obeying the law!" Yes, it is strange, isn't it!

If you ever feel that way, or even guilty about nothing, this discussion will probably resonate with you.

Decades ago, in fact it was 1973, a very funny piece in *The Christian Science Monitor* was written by a witty columnist named Melvin Maddocks. Under the title, "Don't point the finger," he wrote, "Supply a psychic vacuum; guilt will fill it." He said it's the reason twenty cars pull over to the side of the road, when a police car sounds its siren.

Explaining that young children haven't yet learned guilt, and that the very elderly have either forgotten or no longer care, he concluded the rest of us have a problem. This is portrayed in a dialogue between the self and guilt.

Guilt (sternly): Hey, you there!
Self: Who, me?
Guilt: Yes, you.
Self: Why?
Guilt: Don't you know why?
Self (guilty): Yes, I guess I do.
Guilt: Good man! I knew you'd think of something.

Let's note that Melvin prefaced his piece with "supply a physic vacuum." Interesting! It sounds as though when thinking takes a vacation, guilt fills the mental space. After all, there's the old saying that nature abhors a vacuum. Let's investigate what actually is going on here.

The Book of John records the introduction of Jesus by him who prepared the way for the Messiah. Yes, it was John the Baptist, who heralded the transition that was being made from the old covenant with God to the new. This appears in John. (1:15-17)

> John bare witness of him, and cried, saying, This was he of whom I spake, He that cometh after me is preferred before me: for he was before me.

> And of his fulness have all we received, and grace for grace.
>
> For the law was given by Moses, but grace and truth came by Jesus Christ.

The Mosaic law, seen in the Ten Commandments, is an indispensable part of our journey Spiritward. It's a strong rock upon which to launch our boat out onto the waters of spiritual progress. But humanity often lingers on that spot, without moving on to the next stage, which is the blessedness found in Jesus' Sermon on the Mount. When arriving there, we are likely to view that police car with joy and gratitude. "Oh, look, I have a symbol of law and order right here beside me in traffic. How grateful I am for that!" We do need to move on to that blessedness, for the law by itself can make us feel guilty.

We may even toggle back and forth between those two emotions, guilt and gratitude. Planting our feet securely on the forward path is the challenge. It's worth investigating the way Paul gives us out of this predicament, for the tendency to feel guilty detracts from one's joy and productivity. Undeserved self-condemnation and guilt will even hamper our ability to heal, according to Mary Baker Eddy. This makes it doubly important to oust guilt.

Paul helps us to cancel the guilt trip, with all its accusations and self-condemnation. Due to our appearance, and how we are clothed, we might appear guilty, but Paul tells us otherwise.

The law was designed to align us with the one God, Spirit, and to prevent errant fleshly, human behavior. Paul tells us we won't feel condemned or guilty just because it appears we are, at this moment, clothed in "sinful flesh."

The chalk numbers on the chalkboard are not the real numbers. Likewise, the flesh (the chalk of us) is not the real of us. We just don't have to go along with it, believe it, or identify with it.

Opposed to all the human hypotheses, conjectures and opinions about mankind, the scientific statement of being states, "Spirit is God, and man is His image and likeness. Therefore man is not material; he is spiritual." (S&H 468)

Many accounts today of people overcoming great difficulties will attest to that. They have walked or talked despite medical verdicts to the contrary. They have found out, at least to some degree, that the body isn't who they truly are, and it can't limit or define them. As one such woman emphatically exclaimed to her audience, "I'm not my body, and you are not yours either!"

If we agree with that, and don't agree with the concept that flesh defines us, then we won't feel condemned or guilty, as Paul tells us.

> There is therefore now no condemnation to them which are in Christ Jesus, who walk not after the flesh, but after the Spirit. (Romans 8:1)

Secondly, he states the obvious. People pursue the things in which they are invested, or most interested, either the material or the spiritual.

> For they that are after the flesh do mind the things of the flesh; but they that are after the Spirit the things of the Spirit. (Romans 1:5)

Then Paul warns that if our interests are in the material, physical aspects of living, we won't be alive enough to appreciate what life truly is.

> For to be carnally minded is death; but to be spiritually minded is life and peace. (Romans 1:6)

Spiritually minded and carnally (fleshly) minded are totally incompatible. They just don't get along!

> Because the carnal mind is enmity against God: for it is not subject to the law of God, neither indeed can be. So then they that are in the flesh cannot please God. (Romans 1:7,8)

But, happily, we are not relegated to, or lost in, that error of belief about life, for we can choose to live in the spiritual sense of life.

> But ye are not in the flesh, but in the Spirit, if so be that the Spirit of God dwell in you. (Romans 1:9)

The Spirit of God enables us to obey the Ten Commandments while fulfilling the Beatitudes, the state of blessedness. We feel blessed and want to bless others too. Signs of this progress are when we view the good around us and give gratitude for it. Yes, even for the police car on the road.

When out walking, I watched as a man went up in a bucket, from the truck he was driving, to replace a street light bulb. He was a one-man repair service, and I thanked him for it. What we so often take for granted are actually wonderful instances of divine Love's provision for us on the human scene. Every time such gratitude wells up in us, we can be sure we are entering the state of blessedness. Then something becomes very obvious. Guilt and gratitude do not exist together. One cancels out the other.

Blessedness has absolutely nothing to do with how the body looks or feels, because flesh does not factor into true being. Paul was very emphatic about this topic, and this time to the Corinthians. "Now this I say, brethren, that flesh and blood cannot inherit the kingdom of God." (1 Cor. 15:50)

It's impossible to drag along finite, limited, mortal, fleshly, material beliefs about life into the spiritual dimension of infinite, unlimited goodness, and blessedness.

Just ask a group of people to describe themselves and they may very well tell what kind of a person they are. Some might claim to be industrious, patient, kind, honest and so forth, or even the opposite. The body isn't a sufficient description for anyone, and most of us already know this, when willing to admit it. Perhaps humanity is further along than we might suspect in this regard.

How we identify ourselves is the question. For instance, when someone is interested in my age, I'm likely to give the following explanation.

"I'm masquerading as a senior citizen. The reason is, because I'm in the witness protection program. And if you want to know why, it's because I've seen too much of human life and am about to blow the whistle on it!" By that time, we're laughing and the person has forgotten their question.

Seriously, it all comes down to a correct identification. Paul doesn't want us to identify ourselves as sinning mortals, good mortals, as young or old mortals. He's saying we should walk in and with the Spirit. Learn to identify with the spiritual, not the material. Learn to love all impartially. That's the state of blessedness to be in!

The truth is man always has been, and always will be, the precious, beloved, guiltless, sinless, spiritual child of a perfect Father-Mother, God.

While we are happy to be off the guilt trip, we still need to answer the following question, if not for our own, for the world's sake. So, let's tackle it.

Are we all sinners?

What a millstone to hang around the neck of humanity, to tell them that they are all sinners! Unfortunately, that is exactly what most religions have done over the centuries, with the promise of hellfire as a consequence. It's an imposition placed on humankind, but with a vague possibility of salvation from this imposition. It's like saying, "I've placed this label on you, but perhaps, I may be able to take it off for you."

The problem is that it's been unrecognized as pure speculation. It was the filling in of details that we've talked about. Again, perhaps well intended, but nevertheless erroneous.

My husband Glen told me of a woman he was reassuring by telling her she was not a sinner. He said it four times, and each time she agreed, by replying, "I know; I'm not." On the fifth time, she burst into tears and said, "I wish I could believe that!" She had wanted to take that label off herself, but it remained invisibly and securely attached, for it was an early church teaching she had received.

Where did this teaching originate? It had to be from the Adam and Eve story. Due to this allegory, one of the most strongly held beliefs by orthodox Christianity is that we are all sinners and need to be saved. It's a basic teaching. But how correct is it, and why should there be any doubt about its authenticity?

The greatest challenge to this teaching comes from Jesus' own words, when he was chastised by the Pharisees for dining with publicans and sinners. "They that are whole need not a physician; but they that are sick. I came not to call the righteous, but sinners to repentance," was his reply. (Luke 5:31)

Here, and in two other Gospels recounting the same event, Jesus is making a distinction between the righteous and sinners. Obviously, there were two classes of people, and one only needed his help. He was the physician for the sick in body and for those who enacted "sick" deeds, the sinners. He was not attempting to reform the righteous. They were on a good path already.

Jesus did not call everyone sinners! So, how can we?!

It's the "sinful flesh" as Paul calls it, which is the problem that keeps cropping up. But that sinful flesh is a general belief held by those in the flesh. Some participate in it wholeheartedly and add a specific sin to the generic sin. Individuals, who do righteously, are not specifically sinners.

So, are we all sinners? Generically, yes we are, due to the appearance of being clothed in "sinful flesh." But no, we are not, if we are not specifically sinning.

Let's talk about the temptation to do wrong for a moment, as temptation is often the source of guilt.

We may have temptations come to us, as they did to Jesus, but that of itself doesn't make one guilty, or a sinner. Those temptations are in the general atmosphere waiting to be picked up as a signal on someone's mental radar. They are only suggestions, just as the thought that four times two can be nine is a suggestion. There's no substance to a temptation. Unless we are immersing ourselves in wrong thinking and doing, we haven't invited the temptation to come. It's what we do with the temptation, accept it or dismiss it, which is the indicator of the presence or absence of sin. We can resist any specific sin that comes to us.

Our own sinful tendencies, that we do invite or indulge in, have to be dealt with and strongly. Those we need to own up to and challenge. We can't overlook them by declaring the divine fact that there is no sin. We have to prove that humanly, just as we prove a mathematical fact. Let's compare the real and the unreal that way, and use mathematics to explain it.

The first chapter of Genesis is like the invisible, real numbers. (It's the divine reality.) This is where man is made in the image and likeness of God, Spirit. In this account, man and the universe are entirely spiritual.

The second chapter is like the chalk numbers on the chalkboard. (It's the human scene.) This second account of man made from the dust is the story of chalk numbers, which can be erased.

Nothing happens to the real, invisible numbers no matter what takes place on the chalkboard.

Furthermore, while the invisible math numbers never make mistakes or do wrong, that is not true about the chalk numbers. Much mathematical mayhem may take place on the chalkboard.

Affirming we are all born into sin is like saying we're all born into chalk and will make math mistakes. Humanly speaking, that may be generally correct, but it's not specifically true at all. The chalk numbers don't have to take part in the woes of wrong mathematics. They can refuse to do so.

The general belief, called the flesh, is a sinful, material, limited concept of life, in which all appear to participate. It is opposed to the spiritual sense of life.

The main proponent of that sinful sense of life is supposedly a man called Adam. That name was given to the erroneous belief of life in matter in the same way a name, either male or female, is given to a hurricane. Just as a point of interest, female names were formerly used, but now male and female names are rotated. At least this hurricane-naming is now an equal-opportunity honor, if one can call it that.

Adam is a generic title given to the swirling, stormy, erroneous and destructive beliefs about life, and is not the story of one specific man at all. That's true, though Paul said, again to the Romans, that "For as by one man's disobedience many were made sinners, so by the obedience of one shall many be made righteous." (Rom. 5:19) We can reason it out.

This has to be a general statement about disobedience, because no one individual could have literally created multitudes of sinners. There is no pass-me-down sin. It's a metaphor, not a human occurrence. Those participating in the story belong to the "sinning race of Adam." (S&H 345)

One man's disobedience refers to accepting the erroneous concept of material life and creatorship. Biting into that apple of false knowledge has produced crowds of sinners and wrecked countless lives. It's a storm that hasn't died down yet.

However, many were saved by accepting the true sense of life through one man's obedience, which refers specifically to Jesus.

Christ Jesus made no distinction between those who could or could not be saved from that storm. No special class of Christian was favored. To be born again was a spiritual demand on humanity to release the material, fleshly concept of life—throw away the rotten apple. All could participate in that right endeavor.

A proportional exit from the flesh, with its sinful beliefs, is taking place as we turn increasingly to God, Spirit, and walk on that spiritual path. And there is no condemnation due those who are progressively making that exit, even though the flesh is still in evidence—though the chalk hangs around for awhile—until we can do all our mathematics mentally, and our true spiritual selfhood is revealed.

What Jesus taught

Many in today's scientific era may not even consider the Bible relevant. It is difficult to accept the promises, made by some religions, such as Jesus' personal return to earth. That's only one reason why a key to the Bible is necessary, to resolve those difficulties. Another reason may be rather surprising to us, though in a way we already know this.

Jesus didn't detail out his healing method or attach in-depth explanations to his teachings. In fact, he most often used parables, and on a few occasions he would explain those to his disciples. Surely, no Bible scholar would deny that was the case. Jesus did not deal in specifics.

Under the paragraph heading, "A definite rule discovered" in *Science and Health*, we find:

> Our Master healed the sick, practised Christian healing, and taught the generalities of its divine Principle to his students; but he left no definite rule for demonstrating this Principle of healing and preventing disease. This rule remained to be discovered in Christian Science. (S&H 147)

Jesus taught generalities! We could say that he fully illustrated the big picture, the power of Spirit over matter, and in so many different ways.

He turned the water into wine, and healed the blind, the lame, and the leper. Defying the laws of physics, Jesus was able to be instantly at his destination. As we know, he gave sermons to the crowds, which he later fed by spiritual means alone.

We don't have a record of all he said, but it seemed more than enough for mankind at the time. Jesus himself declared it.

> I have yet many things to say unto you, but ye cannot bear them now. Howbeit when he, the Spirit of truth, is come, he will guide you into all truth: for he shall not speak of himself; but whatsoever he shall hear, that shall he speak: and he will shew you things to come. (John 16:12,13)

He promised that details, and even prophecies, would have to come later and comfort the waiting hearts. As usual, human thought rushed to fill in the big picture with its own speculations. The world had to wait 2,000 years for the details that Jesus promised to be published for all to understand.

Right here, we have a perfect instance of the generic and the specific, and the necessity of having both in order to fully understand the subject. Christ Jesus taught the generalities of the Principle of his healing method, and Christian Science brought the specifics.

A promised comfort

Christ Jesus obviously knew the specifics of what he was practicing and teaching would need to be revealed to humanity at some point. That's why he promised that the Comforter would come and explain it all—tell and teach the details. (John 14)

> These things have I spoken unto you, being yet present with you. But the Comforter, which is the Holy Ghost, whom the Father will send in my name, he shall teach you all things, and bring all things to your remembrance, whatsoever I have said unto you.

Jesus also said the Comforter would be with us always. "And I will pray the Father, and he shall give you another Comforter, that he may abide with you for ever." A person couldn't be with us forever, but a divine Principle and a divine Science could. He also warned that if he didn't go away, the Comforter would not come.

How logical that is! For example, if we rely on a great math teacher personally, we won't be able to work out the math rules ourselves. That comfort of understanding just won't come to us.

It has been said by some scholars that the Bible is sufficient, and that if it were well enough understood *Science and Health* would not have been needed.

But that reasoning doesn't hold true in the light of Jesus' promise. It also overlooks the fact that the specifics are requisite. So, if we trust the Bible, then we'll trust Jesus' promise of the Comforter too.

Yes, the Bible is our sufficient guide to eternal life, but in order to follow that guide, we'll need to understand exactly what is being said. Jesus promised that specific comfort would be brought to humanity at the right time and in God's own way.

Students of Christian Science understand the Comforter to be divine Science, and that Science, applied to humanity's needs, is named Christian Science. It's the knowledge of practical Christianity, the path Jesus was showing us.

This makes such sense on many levels. We all feel a great sense of comfort when we understand something. It's important to gain the details of any worthwhile endeavor. For instance, there's a world of difference in playing the piano by ear and knowing the rules of music, how to read music, to follow the correct timing and value of individual notes.

The Gospel of John is the only one that prophesies the coming Comforter. The other three Gospels instead explain, in parable fashion, the second coming of Jesus as the glorious descent of an individual to earth.

How to reconcile John's record with those of Matthew, Mark and Luke is possible if we approach it from the standpoint that they are all talking about the same event, just from a different perspective.

The version in the three Gospels sounds as though it depicts a literal person, while John's version is impersonal.

In this context of the second coming, Jesus stated, "Heaven and earth shall pass away, but my words shall not pass away." (Matt.24:35) He also said that the Comforter would bring all things to our remembrance. Obviously, this Comforter was more than simply a reminder to us of his words. Humanity would be comforted with the understanding of those words and the specifics of his teaching.

Of course, these accounts are all given in Jesus' own words, and it's important to remember he spoke figuratively or in parables. The Son of Man coming in clouds of glory might simply imply that the glorious truths he taught would come to earth again and sort it all out for us, for he used the analogy of sorting sheep from goats as a result of that coming.

The sorting is not about animals but refers to types of thinking, which Jesus explains in terms of compassion for others. Are we going to be sheep, who follow the true path of love, or will we be goats that refuse to budge or notice anyone else's need?

It's helpful to read such versions as in Matthew 25 from that point of view, as kinds of thinking. All wrong thinking (not people) will be banished and burnt up (everlasting fire). Errors of thinking must be burned up in the fires of progress, while the righteous thoughts receive eternal life because they are of God. The Comforter explains it all to us!

Will Jesus return to earth?

Reasoning it out impersonally as we just have, it does not appear that Jesus will return again in the flesh. But if we doubt that reasoning, we can tackle it again and find the answer in the words of the Bible. This helps us solve the question of why we so often wait around for good things to happen.

Will Jesus come again and in the flesh? No, he won't, according to what Paul taught. Let's follow his line of reasoning, step by step.

Was Jesus sinless? Yes, specifically!
"For we have not an high priest which cannot be touched with the feeling of our infirmities; but was in all points tempted like as we are, yet without sin." (Hebrews 4:15)

Did Jesus appear clothed in "sinful flesh?" Yes!
"For what the law could not do, in that it was weak through the flesh, God sending his own Son in the likeness of sinful flesh, and for sin, condemned sin in the flesh." (Romans 8:3)

Will he come again in the flesh? No!
"So Christ was once offered to bear the sins of many; and unto them that look for him shall he appear the second time without sin unto salvation." (Hebrews 9:28)

The second appearance will be without sin, but the first appearance was also without sin. Is this a contradiction? Not at all, if we apply the generic and specific differences.

The first appearance was without sin because Jesus was a sinless individual, who made no errors or mistakes in his demonstration of his divine nature, the Christ. He was specifically sinless.

However, he was clothed with the flesh, the general sinful belief that life is limited, is in matter, and subject to decay and death. So, generically Jesus' physical appearance was with sin, while his whole career was specifically sinless.

The second coming will be without sin, without that fleshy belief, so he will not come again in the flesh, but appear in the understanding. His teaching is illustrated again to us through the Comforter, divine Science.

The following example may be considered as going from the sublime to the ridiculous, though I wouldn't put a sweet baby bird in the latter category.

As mentioned, when my husband Glen and I lived on Palomar Mountain, we learned many wonderful spiritual lessons. One of these was in the form of a little bird that came, actually walked, to our home and stayed with us awhile. We simply called him Bird, and that's the title of a book about him.

It's a beautiful, true story. When the book was published years after this experience, it was as though Bird had come once again.

The first time, he appeared "in the feathers" (that is, when they grew in). The second time he appeared without the feathers, in a book so all can read about the lessons he taught us. He can be understood through that book.

In fact, a Christian Science nurse told me that a medical nurse friend of hers, who was going in the direction of Christian Science, had read the book and applied the spiritual truths that shone through the story, to the case of a mother and her premature baby, with healing as a result. Yes, Bird in his current form can stay with us forever.

Let's just emphasize the main points again, as they are of inestimable value. If you find any of this repetitious, it is only for more clarity on the subject, as we all read and understand things in different ways. So, it can be of great advantage to restate vital concepts.

Jesus came the first time clothed in the flesh, a sinful concept of life, a generic one, but he was specifically sinless.

The second time he would come without sin, without "sinful flesh." Therefore, it was not a person who would appear again, but Jesus' teaching with the specifics explained. What a comfort to have that explanation! The coming of the Comforter, revealing the divine Science of Life, is the second coming of Jesus. Mary Baker Eddy discovered this Science, on which Jesus' based his words and works, and named it Christian Science.

For Jesus to appear in the flesh is similar to writing a number in chalk on the chalkboard. We all know that's a temporary, erasable appearance and not the real number at all. Trying to pass off the chalk as the real thing would be to tell a lie about the true number, which is not erasable. That's why flesh is sinful, because it's a lie about true spiritual being.

Jesus will not need to appear again in the flesh (in the chalk). The real need is to have the truth he taught and practiced available and understood. The Comforter does that very thing!

Let us think for a moment what this one change in religious understanding and teaching would mean to all mankind. No hoping and waiting for a person to come and save us. No waiting around for good to happen sometime in our lives. It's present here and now. That teaching about Jesus basically put good on hold, and hit the pause button for humanity.

Paul proclaimed the present, timeless availability of all that is truly good, and *Science and Health*, on page 39, provides the specifics.

> "*Now*," cried the apostle, "is the accepted time; behold, *now* is the day of salvation," — meaning, not that now men must prepare for a future-world salvation, or safety, but that now is the time in which to experience that salvation in spirit and in life.

The importance of place

How important is it to understand the place Jesus held? If the Council of Nicaea is any indicator of that, we would have to say it is of vital importance to the world and to us.

The place of Jesus was hotly debated by two opposing viewpoints. He was the Son of God or he was God. Orthodox Christianity preaches the latter.

That Council of Nicaea took place in 325 A.D. and it is no coincidence that something happened to healing right around that time. It was lost!

> The proofs of Truth, Life, and Love, which Jesus gave by casting out error and healing the sick, completed his earthly mission; but in the Christian Church this demonstration of healing was early lost, about three centuries after the crucifixion. (S&H 41)

Mrs. Eddy said that it was Jesus' theology that healed the sick. Central to his theology was a relationship. He expressed the Christ, the spiritual idea of sonship. Without sonship, (his and our relationship to God), it would be impossible to heal the sick or the sinning. To mistake his place would cause a ripple effect all the way down the line of thought and affect every part of our own Christian demonstration, healing included.

The same has to be true of Mary Baker Eddy and her place, which has likewise been hotly debated. For her place to be misunderstood would also affect the message she brought and our healing ability. And if we mistrust the messenger, the message will be obscured and less valuable to us.

This point about a right estimate of Christ Jesus and Mrs. Eddy cannot be stressed too much. If that right view of them disappears, the healing disappears. Then the spiritual harmony and health of man, the kingdom of heaven, will never be gained.

About gaining the true idea of the kingdom of heaven in man, Mrs. Eddy wrote, "This goal is never reached while we hate our neighbor or entertain a false estimate of anyone whom God has appointed to voice His Word." (S&H 560)

A mystery to be solved

The centerpiece of Jesus' teaching is undeniably stated in three words by John the beloved disciple, "God is Love." No wonder Mrs. Eddy wrote, "The vital part, the heart and soul of Christian Science, is Love." (S&H 113) Divine Love not only comforts but it heals, as Christian Science has proved for a century and a half.

Those healed of minor or life-threatening illnesses were understandably deeply grateful for their healing, which came as a result of Mary Baker Eddy's discovery of the specifics of Jesus' teaching.

To walk again, hear again, see again, were only a few of the benefits. Lives have been revitalized and made purposeful by this understanding. In the early days, it was said that new students of this Science came from the graveyards. This was true, as cases pronounced hopeless by the medical faculty were healed through Christian Science.

So, when the circumstances surrounding her discovery appeared to parallel those of the woman depicted in the twelfth chapter of Revelation (termed the Apocalypse around 1150 A.D.), a connection was made and the idea proposed that Mary Baker Eddy was that woman. But was she? What did that mean?

Instead of jumping straight into the fray or to conclusions (this mystery has a surprise ending), let's back up a little and follow a chain of spiritual events.

To begin with, there was strong, even undeniable, evidence that Jesus came in accordance with prophecies about him, made by people such as Isaiah and Micah. The angel message which comforted Joseph when he found out Mary, his betrothed, was expecting a child, reminded him of that fact.

Indeed, this was a very specific prophecy about the human appearing of Jesus, and his birth was pinpointed exactly. It was to take place in Bethlehem. Further events of his life, and even the crucifixion, were likewise foretold.

But there was no such prophecy about a specific woman, a human being, though there were general references to woman, such as the one made by Jesus to a woman leavening three measures of meal.

By no means, does this suggest that woman has no vital part to play in Truth's advent on earth, and the spiritual scene is not complete without her.

A symbol of Love

Immediately after quoting Revelation 12:1, which told of a "great wonder in heaven; a woman clothed with the sun," Mary Baker Eddy wrote in *Science and Health* about the necessity to have a correct sense of those whom God appoints "to voice His Word." It's under the paragraph heading, "True estimate of God's messenger." (S&H 560)

In that same paragraph, she stated: "The botanist must know the genus and species of a plant in order to classify it correctly. As it is with things, so is it with persons." This is a very large clue, for she is asking us to classify persons generically and specifically too. That sounds surprising, doesn't it!

Let's think about that for a few moments. The genus and the species are often described in words such as general, generic, or generically and then specific or specifically.

Intuitively hoping for a correct classification for her, students of Christian Science have mightily endeavored to accord to Mary Baker Eddy her proper due and her rightful place.

But how do we do that? We follow all the clues the Bible and her writings provide for us. No opinions! Let's approach this all-important subject in a few different ways. If one way doesn't resonate with all of us, then another very well might.

The Bible attaches no human designation to the woman in the Apocalypse, and neither does Mary Baker Eddy. Actually, it was quite the opposite, as Mrs. Eddy described her as a symbol, not a person.

That woman was to illustrate a wonderful fact of a universe governed by divine Principle, Love. Its own spiritual idea of love expresses this Principle.

> The woman in the Apocalypse symbolizes generic man, the spiritual idea of God; she illustrates the coincidence of God and man as the divine Principle and divine idea. (S&H 561)

Furthermore, the symbol of a woman was needed to reveal the motherhood of God and so complete the idea of the Godhead.

> As Elias presented the idea of the fatherhood of God, which Jesus afterwards manifested, so the Revelator completed this figure with woman, typifying the spiritual idea of God's motherhood. (S&H 562)

GUIDEBOOK INFORMATION

Now, Jesus came *to fulfill* prophecy. Jesus was prophesied about specifically. His name was given and place of birth. The entire description of Jesus coming, and even his life, was specific.

Mary Baker Eddy came *and fulfilled* prophecy. Mrs. Eddy was not prophesied about specifically. The woman in the Apocalypse was a general prophecy of a woman, not a specific one, for she symbolized generic man, a spiritual type of man, God's idea. Mrs. Eddy represented that idea of woman.

Perhaps, you might agree that this is a correct classification for both Jesus and Mary Baker Eddy, but if you don't, we can still reason this out further by following more clues.

Jesus arrived *with the understanding* of his true nature, the Christ. He came to bear witness to the Christ, Truth. He tells us that in John 18:37.

> To this end was I born, and for this cause came I into the world, that I should bear witness unto the truth.

Mary Baker Eddy arrived *without the understanding* of Christian Science and had to discover it. She was God-prepared and God-appointed to carry that message to the world.

> Has God entrusted me with a message to mankind? — then I cannot choose but obey. (Mess. '01, 31)

Let's recap for a moment in another way. Mary Baker Eddy was definitely God-appointed. She wasn't just some spiritually-minded, intelligent woman, who happened to catch sight of a great truth, as the tallest tree would receive the first rays of the rising sun. No, she was chosen and specifically appointed by God "to voice His word," just as Jesus was appointed to bear witness to the Truth.

To believe that Mrs. Eddy was simply "the tallest tree" would be to leave her out of her place in Revelation, out of prophecy. This was unacceptable to students of Christian Science. But to believe she was the actual woman in the Apocalypse was not really acceptable to everyone either. It appeared that either "she is **or** she isn't."

The dispute over this turned into quite a controversy carrying overtones of the church in Revelation, mentioned by Mrs. Eddy. She wrote that the "Nicolaitan church presents the phase of a great controversy, ready to destroy the unity and the purity of the church." (Mess. '00:12)

Though the debate is now relatively dormant, the need for a viable solution still remains. Perhaps asking a pivotal question about Jesus and Mary Baker Eddy will further help solve the mystery.

They were both appointed by God, but **when** were they appointed? Jesus, having been foreseen and expected, was appointed **before** he arrived on the human scene. Mary Baker Eddy was appointed **after** she arrived. This is easy to reason out.

If Mary Baker Eddy had been appointed—foreseen and expected—before her birth, she would have arrived with the understanding of the Science, just as Jesus arrived with his understanding of the Christ. But she didn't. She had to discover it here. And this would explain why she doesn't fill the place of a witness, but rather of a messenger.

Yes, God entrusted Mary Baker Eddy with the message. God appointed her to carry out this mission. But she was appointed after she arrived on the human scene and not before. Jesus was appointed before he arrived. Again, he came *to fulfill* prophecy. She came *and fulfilled* prophecy.

She was appointed to "give birth" to another witness to the Truth, that would be complementary to the witnessing of Jesus.

These are the two witnesses spoken of in the eleventh chapter of Revelation, "And I will give power unto my two witnesses." Mrs. Eddy identifies them this way.

> Science and Health makes it plain to all Christian Scientists that the manhood and womanhood of God have already been revealed in a degree through Christ Jesus and Christian Science, His two witnesses. (My 346)

Let's note that Mrs. Eddy is not personally the witness, but her discovery is. Though inseparable from her discovery, and therefore from the witness, she is not synonymous with it.

One cannot exchange the two, her name and the discovery's name, and still be correct in their understanding of Christian Science. In fact, that is one of the major mistakes made in this department of investigation.

To recap: the woman in the Apocalypse is a symbol. She (a) symbolizes generic man, (b) illustrates the divine coincidence, and (c) typifies the idea of God's motherhood. She is used for all three for a reason:

> In divine Science, we have not as much authority for considering God masculine, as we have for considering Him feminine, for Love imparts the clearest idea of Deity. (S&H 517)

Here is the obvious point of agreement between John's declaration, "God is Love" and that of Christian Science which states, "Love imparts the clearest idea of Deity."

There are a number of synonyms for God, but only one is both specific and generic. "Love is the generic term for God." (My. 185)

Now, it would surely follow that if Love is the generic term for God, then God's idea, or generic man, would be symbolized by a woman. And that's exactly how Mrs. Eddy defined the woman in the Apocalypse, as symbolizing generic man.

That woman is a symbol of a divine idea, not a symbol of a human woman, and she illustrates a divine fact, a divine concept, and just as with any concept, one may fulfill it on the human scene, but not actually be it. Even Jesus, though inseparable from the Christ, was not synonymous with it.

Likewise, Mary Baker Eddy is inseparable from, but not synonymous with, divine Science. The human temptation is to make the human synonymous with, or equal to, the divine. But, "The divine must overcome the human at every point." (S&H 43)

Mary Baker Eddy's life showed a startling similarity to the events surrounding the woman in the Apocalypse. The woman brought forth "a man child" to rule the world. Mary Baker Eddy brought forth a divine Science, showing God's government of the universe and man. For "Christ, God's idea, will eventually rule all nations...with divine Science." (S&H 565)

The resistance to the "man child," the divine idea the woman brought forth, was also very evident in Mrs. Eddy's life as she had to endure persecution, slander and outright attacks on her discovery of divine Science. Her experiences truly paralleled those of the woman, when evil was seen as a flood seeking to sweep away the spiritual truth that was being brought to the material world.

Jesus knew that would happen. He had already told and foretold of the persecution the followers of Truth would suffer. He knew the Comforter, divine Science, would incur mighty resistance and upheavals of thought, yes, even of earthquake proportion. People, of high and low rank, would hide from the truth, "in the rocks of the mountains."

Mary Baker Eddy fulfilled Jesus' promise to the world, that it would receive the Comforter. She also fulfilled the description of the woman in the Apocalypse. She represented that woman. So, was she actually that woman? What does this question even mean?

If it is proposed that Mary Baker Eddy came to fulfill prophecy in the same manner as did Jesus, with her human appearing likewise being foretold, (which it wasn't) then we would have to answer "no." She is not that woman. Also, had that been the case, she would have arrived with Christian Science and not had to discover it.

If we conclude that Mrs. Eddy, as the God-prepared and God-appointed messenger, did indeed fulfill the prophecies regarding that woman, then we would answer "yes." In one way, she is the woman in the Apocalypse, and in another way she isn't.

It was never "is **or** isn't," but "is **and** is not."

She is, and she isn't. How is that possible? You may recall the argument about one man or many men. The same solution applies to this problem. The answer will vary according to the view, for the frame of reference cannot be omitted, or else we would have a one-sided picture.

So, was Mary Baker Eddy the woman in the Apocalypse? Generically, yes! Specifically, no!

If we aren't totally convinced at this point that the woman in the Apocalypse did not refer specifically to the human being, Mary Baker Eddy, there is still another way we can reason this out. The argument in this case will be irrefutable.

I hope, dear reader, you are not tiring of this subject, because resolving it would be invaluable to us all. Just think of the effect of repairing any broken bonds of brotherhood, not to mention helping the Cause and future of Christian Science!

It's a coincidence!

The idea of the woman in the Apocalypse being a symbol and not a specific woman, though a specific woman was chosen to represent her, explains both (a) generic man and (c) the motherhood of God.

Perhaps, (c) is somewhat akin to the Statue of Liberty which, as Mrs. Eddy wrote, has "no physical antecedent." That statue stands for an idea, not a person, but if it were to be expressed humanly, a woman would obviously be chosen for that part.

We could turn our attention now to (b) the second statement about the woman, that she "illustrates the coincidence of God and man as the divine Principle and divine idea." On that same page 561 is a similar reference, and this time to do with Jesus.

John saw the human and divine coincidence, shown in the man Jesus, as divinity embracing humanity in Life and its demonstration, — reducing to human perception and understanding the Life which is God.

Jesus showed the coincidence, a coming together, a coinciding or agreement of the human with the divine. We might think in terms of a chalkboard. When the chalk on the board agrees with the invisible principle of mathematics, we can say they coincide, or agree. Jesus presented true humanhood in that he was sinless, for he was in perfect agreement with his Principle, divine Love.

However, there is another and higher coincidence, which is when the invisible number coincides with its principle. This number, an idea, is not expressed in chalk.

Likewise, the coincidence seen in the woman in the Apocalypse is not a human coincidence but a divine one, for she "illustrates the coincidence of God and man as the divine Principle and divine idea."

One coincidence is of the human and the divine, and the higher is the coincidence of divine Principle and divine idea. The human does not appear at all in that divine-with-divine coincidence.

That's one reason Mary Baker Eddy, a human being, could not specifically be that woman, and here is another.

Jesus, according to Christian Science, was the "highest human corporeal concept of the divine idea." (S&H 589)

For any human woman to be that woman in the Apocalypse would mean that she was higher than the "highest human corporeal concept," higher than Jesus, because the coincidence of divine with divine is higher than that of the human and the divine. How impossible to be higher than the highest!

Let's just restate that concept using an equation. Math facts and terms are often quite helpful in explaining metaphysical truths. We might use an equal sign to mean "illustrates."

Jesus = human + divine coincidence.

Woman in the Apocalypse = divine idea + divine Principle coincidence.

The first coincidence includes human and divine.

The second coincidence is higher than the first, because it is the divine with the divine.

Jesus was the "highest human corporeal concept of the divine idea." He demonstrated, Christ, Truth.

The woman in the Apocalypse could not refer to a human being (higher than Jesus) in the divine with the divine equation.

All of which brings us back to the conclusion that Mary Baker Eddy was generically, but not specifically, the woman in the Apocalypse.

Everyone should rest easy, because everyone was correct, but only in one sense. The students who argued that Mary Baker Eddy was the woman in the Apocalypse were correct generically. The ones who argued she was not the woman were correct specifically. Now, isn't that a happy resolution to a sticky problem?!

The clue was there all along in the words *genus* and *species* on page 560, where it is explained that Truth and Love will be hidden from us if the messenger is misunderstood. How important it is to value and acknowledge Mrs. Eddy's true place!

The results of acknowledging woman

As previously stated, it's vital to our healing work to gain and maintain a right estimate of both Christ Jesus and Mary Baker Eddy and their place in prophecy. That will preserve healing, and accomplish even more, because Christian Science is the *key* witness for the motherhood of God.

As mankind acknowledges God's motherhood, then a united Father-Mother, no longer incomplete nor divorced by human concepts, will be apparent. A new era will blossom, in which love increasingly becomes the motivator of mankind. The worldwide view and treatment of girls and women will change for the better. It's inevitable! Women will walk out of the bondage imposed by false belief and customs, and men will join them in a new freedom.

This progressive era is already taking shape in many ways, and is being articulated openly. On a Larry King TV special some years ago, he interviewed a number of clergy, including a Catholic priest and Marianne Williamson. They all readily agreed that God is Mother as well as Father.

You may recall the hit song "Let the River Run" by Carly Simon. The last two verses are rather surprising, for they welcome the new Jerusalem and freedom for all, both sons and daughters.

> We're coming to the edge
> Running on the water
> Coming through the fog
> Your sons and daughters
>
> Let the river run
> Let all the dreamers
> Wake the nation
> Come, the new Jerusalem

Gihon, the river that flowed out of Eden, will be well traveled. This river of thought is defined as: "The rights of woman acknowledged morally, civilly, and socially." (S&H 587)

Paul had a clear sense of the new Jerusalem and must have glimpsed God's motherhood. The International Standard Version of Galatians 4:26 records him as saying, "But the heavenly Jerusalem is the free woman, and she is our spiritual mother."

St. John saw the holy city, the new Jerusalem, as a "bride coming down from God out of heaven." (Revelation 21:2)

Mary Baker Eddy defined New Jerusalem as Divine Science, which she, a woman, discovered.

At the 1895 dedication of The Mother Church in Boston, many newspapers carried articles and commentaries. One such newspaper was *The New Century* with a wonderful piece titled, "One point of view—the new woman." (Pulpit and Press 81-84)

Speaking of woman generically and symbolically, the male reporter wrote these stirring words:

> We rejoice with her that at last we begin to know what John on Patmos meant— "And there appeared a great wonder in heaven, a woman clothed with the sun, and the moon under her feet, and upon her head a crown of twelve stars.". . . "The time of times" is near when "the new woman" shall subdue the whole earth with the weapons of peace. Then shall wrong be robbed of her bitterness and ingratitude of her sting, revenge shall clasp hands with pity, and love shall dwell in the tents of hate; while side by side, equal partners in all that is worth living for, shall stand the new man with the new woman.

This reporter, with knowledge of the Scriptures, saw woman's emergence as a prophecy of love taking the lead. How wonderful!

GUIDEBOOK INFORMATION

A word about travel

When Jesus told us we would know the truth and it would set us free, he gave us the key to salvation—a full salvation from sin, disease and death, here and hereafter.

Do we all need to be saved? Yes, we do, from the general beliefs of the flesh, even if not from specific sins. We are being saved from believing in a lie about life. "This salvation means: saved from error, or error overcome." (Mis. 89)

A very old Star Trek television episode showed a few of the crew holding desperately onto the starship's interior, while all others had been sucked out. It appeared the remaining crew members were in grave danger.

However, as it turned out, the ship was a phantom ship, and they were actually being sucked out to safety. (At least, that's how I recall the episode.) It makes a great point. Sometimes, what we hold onto is totally bogus and a danger to us. It takes courage and willingness to let go.

Even gradually letting go, of a material sense of life in matter, means we'll be welcomed increasingly into the safety of our spiritual life in God, good.

The next question is: What spiritual journey do we need to undertake, in order to flee the dangers of the phantom ship for the safety of the real one?

Let's visit the baseball shop with Earnest Eager and find out!

THE BASEBALL LESSON

Earnest Eager felt exhilarated and inundated at the same time. The information at the kiosk was so plentiful, the answers so available, and the ideas so momentous that he decided to take a walk for a few minutes to digest it all. Then he realized this was not the work of a moment, and that he would have to return again and again to those ideas, which were genuine pearls of wisdom. He was just grateful that he could understand the Guidebook better now, and not adhere to it simply on blind faith. That thought gave him some peace and enabled him to consider the next stage of his quest.

The kiosk attendant was correct in that the baseball shop was only a few doors down on the same side of the road. Earnest pushed open the door and immediately heard the final strains of the baseball song, ". . . three strikes, you're out, at the old ball game." That introduction to the subject wasn't very encouraging, and Earnest hoped he wouldn't strike out with his next clue. Next, he wondered how a clue to life and precious ideas could be in a baseball shop. But he had also begun to realize that important clues could appear in the most unlikely places.

The first thing Earnest glimpsed was a rack of free pamphlets containing the history of baseball. They were titled, "Playing the Game." He tucked one of the pamphlets into his pocket and looked around for a helper.

A young man, appearing to be only in his mid-teens, approached Earnest, who felt uncomfortable, because he didn't really know what to ask about. Hope like a diamond sounded difficult to acquire.

Sensing Earnest's uncertainty and assuming he had a newcomer to the game, the young man first pointed out the baseball equipment. Receiving no positive feedback, he went on to describe the large poster on the wall depicting a baseball field.

At the mention of the baseball diamond, Earnest's face lit up. Seeing his reaction, the attendant pursued that interest by describing the four sides of the diamond, which were all equal, and by explaining that the players had to run every side and touch all the points of the diamond. Even if someone hit the ball really far, maybe out of the park, it was not an automatic homer. That player still had to walk around and touch each base for it to be considered a home run.

Earnest looked like a man who had suddenly heard a click, as the tumblers on a lock fell into place. He had his clue! This was immediately confirmed by the attendant's parting words to him, "That's the great hope! The batters want to make it to home."

A new and higher hope now resided in Earnest Eager's kind heart, and it was to run along the sides of the diamond—to run the bases of life. He may not know yet what each point of that diamond would mean as he touched it, but run he would!

* * * * * * * * * * * * * * * *

The diamond of hope

The beloved disciple John, so close to Jesus, was credited with receiving the Book of Revelation, those divine truths, from Jesus. In chapter 21, John tells of seeing a new heaven and earth.

Mary Baker Eddy, under the title, "One Cause and Effect," wrote in *Miscellaneous Writings*, p.21:

> Christian Science begins with the First Commandment of the Hebrew Decalogue, "Thou shalt have no other gods before me." It goes on in perfect unity with Christ's Sermon on the Mount, and in that age culminates in the Revelation of St. John, who, while on earth and in the flesh, like ourselves, beheld "a new heaven and a new earth," — the spiritual universe, whereof Christian Science now bears testimony.

She had also posed the question:

> The Revelator tells us of "a new heaven and a new earth." Have you ever pictured this heaven and earth, inhabited by beings under the control of supreme wisdom? (S&H 91)

John goes on to relate that, in this new heaven and earth, there is the "new Jerusalem," a city foursquare. A baseball diamond is actually a square with four equal sides, each 90 feet in length. (Tipped on its side, the square becomes a diamond with four points to it.) I find this so helpfully analogous to the city foursquare, a four-sided city with streets of gold. The spiritual universe, and all it contains, is valuable beyond compare, so John uses symbols of gold and precious gems to describe it. After all, we do the same today when we speak of pearls of wisdom.

Science and Health refers to the city foursquare as a "scientific consciousness" and describes, in some detail on pages 574-577, what that entails.

The journey that all of us, who are both earnest and eager, have before us will be to reach that city, the spiritual consciousness where we will not only view, but experience, the new heaven and new earth, the reality, which is the spiritual universe. To do that, we will be traveling the four sides of the city and we'll make sure we touch the important, specific points of it. Yes, we'll need to run the bases.

This puts our life quest for harmony, goodness, and health into a whole new ballpark. No longer do we need to muddle around on a human, mortal playing field that has no real principle or purpose attached to the game. We're not players on some large cosmic game board, thrown randomly onto a field attempting to play a game without rules, and endeavoring, in either good ways or bad, to take care of ourselves, because no one else is going to.

No! In the new venue (the spiritual outlook on life), there is a divine Principle to adhere to, and we find it is divine Love that cares for us. The rules of the game are well defined, and the goal is clear.

Home plate, the true basis of being, is where we begin (we acknowledge the spiritual creation as the real one, and our true, spiritual identity according to the first chapter of Genesis). However, due to the lies told about creation and about us, in the second chapter, we will be required to prove the validity and veracity of the first account. So, we ask in prayer for directions and follow heavenly guidance as we run the bases and prove on the human scene what is divinely true.

There are no shortcuts allowed, no running across the field from first base to third base. The farthermost base or point needs to be touched and the corner or turnaround made correctly before we can arrive at home.

It's no wonder that St. John describes this state of spiritual being as totally harmonious, for "there shall be no more death, neither sorrow, nor crying, neither shall there be any more pain: for the former things are passed away." (Rev. 21:4)

Christ Jesus always preached spiritual ways and means and never pointed to a physical location. With that in mind, let us turn our attention to the travel plan Jesus laid out for us in Revelation.

The pieces come together

First of all, let's assemble what we know and see how the city foursquare, including the diamond, is constructed. There are many pieces given for this puzzle in just a few pages of *Science and Health*.

The sides of the city are the Word, Christ, Christianity and divine Science. The points are the Word of Life, Truth and Love; Christ, the spiritual idea of God; Christianity; and Christian Science.

It doesn't seem wise to attempt any new interpretation than the one given on those pages, but we could make observations about the pieces provided for us. In fact, we could try putting them together in a logical manner, so that we have a plain path to follow. There is a game plan to life, after all!

It appears that the sides of the city foursquare are generic statements of that scientific consciousness, while the points of the city appear to be specific.

THE BASEBALL LESSON

Again, we'll reason it out, not simply take my, or anyone else's, observation as fact.

At first glance, the sides and the points seem to be identical, but they are not. One expands on the other. Let's go around the city on pages 575 and 577 of *Science and Health*.

The Word is the north side and the point expands on that specifically to mean, "the Word of Life, Truth, and Love." Secondly, we have the Christ as a side, and this is specifically "Christ, the spiritual idea of God."

The third side is Christianity. The point is, "Christianity, which is the outcome of the divine Principle of the Christ idea in Christian history."

Lastly, and fourth, is the side of divine Science, the point of which is specifically "Christian Science, which to-day and forever interprets this great example and the great Exemplar."

Regarding the fourth side; when discussing various terms for Science, such as divine Science and Spiritual Science, Mrs. Eddy stated that "Christian Science especially relates to Science as applied to humanity." (S&H 127) For this reason, Christian Science is the more logical specific term than is divine Science, which is more general in its application to human needs.

In each case the specifics of the sides are revealed in the points. That's why it seems reasonable to say that same structure, of generic and specific, is being employed again in this highly symbolic chapter of Revelation.

Why should we tip the square on its side to make it a diamond? Again, this is not a personal interpretation, but rather a structure *Science and Health* gives us, in the form of a spiritual compass.

Directions are necessary for our journey, and are the stars on the north, east, and south. The west has no night star for, at that stage, the morning star, the daystar of divine Science is dawning on our thought. (Preface and page 577) These stars give us our bearings and shine further light of understanding on our journey, so it's possible to ascertain the progress made and the lessons learned. Otherwise, our spiritual path could seem amorphous, without shape or definite direction. Yes, it's easy to track our progress by the points of the spiritual compass.

Let's consider carefully how these stars illumine each spiritual point and highlight the human activity and its results. Speaking of the holy city:

> Northward, its gates open to the North Star, the Word, the polar magnet of Revelation; eastward, to the star seen by the Wisemen of the Orient, who followed it to the manger of Jesus; southward, to the genial tropics, with the Southern Cross in the skies, — the Cross of Calvary, which binds human society into solemn union; westward,

to the grand realization of the Golden Shore of Love and the Peaceful Sea of Harmony. (S&H 575)

There'll be no attempt to have a full discussion of the city foursquare, as it would take too long. (I've given all-day addresses on this one subject alone.) Simply put, Glen and I found that following each side, touching the points, and going around the compass clockwise (unlike the baseball game, which needs to be reversed) provided much needed insight into the spiritual journey facing each one of us.

For instance, there was a time on the mountain when we were deeply invested in studying five translations of the Bible all at once. We were at the north point, the Word of Life, Truth and Love. Shortly after that came some family issues, and we could tell we were on the east and having to apply the ideas of the Christ and true sonship. Shortly after leaving the mountain we purchased a van with conference seating inside and traveled up and down the California coast, on and off for a year, attending various Christian churches and meeting with their pastors. That was definitely the Christian side being more deeply explored. Prior to the mountain, we'd had more insights on the metaphysics of Christian Science (the west point of the city).

It wasn't until afterwards we realized just what had happened, and that it wasn't a one-time-round event. Progress demands we keep traveling around that city. You may recall that Joshua had to encompass Jericho seven times before the walls fell down, and the battle was won.

In like manner, though not counting numerically, it's imperative to do the same with the city foursquare until every wall of false belief, every vestige of belief in life in matter, falls and yields to the reality, and to the perfection of God's creation. Each time we make these rounds, the spiritual truth becomes more obvious and clear and the errors of material sense are less. The pieces are all there and put in order for us. The sides of the city lead to the points, and the stars illumine our pathway and keep us in the right direction.

Perhaps, it would be helpful to give an instance of spiritual lessons on the Christian side that began appearing just before we left the mountain.

One day, Glen suddenly said he thought we should go and visit Earl, the Lutheran pastor who had married us some years previously. We'd seen Earl on and off, as we shared spiritual ideas with him and he with us. Though Glen didn't know why we were going, he just felt we should. Once in Earl's church office, Glen admitted to our friend that we had no idea why we were there. Earl replied he did, and explained that he and two other Christian churches had decided to sponsor meetings and services on the subject of spiritual healing. He humbly admitted they didn't know where to begin, and so he invited us to meet with them in the Methodist church, one of the three involved.

Earl introduced us by saying that Glen and I knew ten times more about healing than they all did, and then amended that to a hundred times more. We were rather surprised at his introduction, but even more taken aback at the reaction of the three clergy. The expectant, humble look on the faces of those three dear men, each with decades of experience in their respective pulpits, was enough to bring tears to one's eyes, and it still is more than thirty years later. Their humility was what we took from that two-hour meeting. Glen and I didn't even recall details of the discussion later on, because their demeanor was really awe-inspiring and made us feel we had much to learn in that department.

In fact, I'm not even sure which of us learned the most that day—the Christians with the Science or the Christians with the humility!

The Christian side of the city, as we explored it, was breathtaking in many ways. If we watch for the city foursquare, then it will become obvious which side or point our lessons in life are on, and the answers we need will be more apparent due to that understanding.

It should go without saying that we are never deprived of any of the four sides or points. They are always all present, no matter which side, or lesson, is requiring our attention at any given moment. It's like being in a certain section of a city that we are exploring. The whole city is always there, and we will make our way around that city many times.

As we pursue the way of the city foursquare something very valuable takes place. This travel will structure our lives, even though we are unaware of it. For instance, that became clear to me years after the *Bird* book was published. I suddenly realized that the four chapters of *Bird* followed each side and point of the city, and in the right order.

Yes, the city foursquare provides us with a perfect travel plan. But, speaking of perfect, how would you feel about telling someone to be perfect? Let's explore this idea next.

Be perfect!

When I was still rather new in the public practice of Christian Science, I was asked to talk with a young man who was taking his name out of church membership. He'd met a group of evangelical Christians who appeared to understand him better.

It all boiled down to the fact that the perfection of man had been emphasized to him at home and in Sunday School, but the encouragement to be on the spiritual journey, to work that out, had been omitted. After all he was a sinner, he told me, and he didn't just mean that generically. He knew that he specifically needed to reform his ways. I don't remember the whole conversation, but he did go ahead and remove his name from the church rolls.

This brings up a question. Would we feel comfortable in urging someone to be perfect like our heavenly Father? We might even want to replace it with a statement as to man's present, spiritual perfection. Perhaps that urging doesn't sound scientific enough or complete? But in the Sermon on the Mount, Jesus had made just such a demand. "Be ye therefore perfect, even as your Father which is in heaven is perfect." (Matthew 5:48)

It would seem Mrs. Eddy was answering an unspoken criticism of that when she wrote, "The divine demand, 'Be ye therefore perfect,' is scientific and intact, and the human footsteps leading to perfection are indispensable." The standpoint is spiritual not human perfection, and we have to run the bases to prove it. She went on to explain this necessity.

> Individuals are consistent who, watching and praying, can "run, and not be weary; . . . walk, and not faint," who gain good rapidly and hold their position, or attain slowly and yield not to discouragement. God requires perfection, but not until the battle between Spirit and flesh is fought and the victory won. (S&H 254)

The great human need is to progress spiritually— to be on our spiritual journey. The starting and finishing points can't be confused, although in baseball they do appear to be the same thing.

Now, here's an observation from someone (me) who knows little about sports, but is often inclined to use them as analogies. The batter starts off at home plate, but has to run the bases and, when he finishes, you might hear the remark made that the runner slid into home or even home base (not plate). He really isn't sliding into home plate as that was his starting not finishing point. What has changed? He has run the bases. He isn't actually at home until that takes place.

In the same way, we might be given the answer to problems in the back of a math book, but are required to work it all out and show how we got there. In other words, we even have to run the mathematical bases before we can claim to have the correct answer. Being aware of and actually proving the answer are two different things.

It seems that the human mind always acts as the loyal (loyal to its own limited beliefs of life and disloyal to the truth) opposition party in such situations. It keeps on claiming to be already there. This is like the entitled dowager who, when asked if she liked to travel, dryly remarked: "Why should I travel; I'm already here!" Of course, divinely we are right here, right now, at the point of perfection, but humanly we are not. In fact, nowhere near it!

Mary Baker Eddy put that argument, that there is no need for spiritual travel, firmly to rest under the title, "Put up thy sword" in *Miscellaneous Writings*, p. 215. She strongly refuted the suggestion we have no bases to run, or no journey to be made in life.

> My students are at the beginning of their demonstration; they have a long warfare with error in themselves and in others to finish, and they must at this stage use the sword of Spirit.
>
> They cannot in the beginning take the attitude, nor adopt the words, that Jesus used at the end of his demonstration.

We can also be kinder to ourselves as we journey on. Expecting to always know the perfect answer to a situation brings only anguish if the answer doesn't appear. Even Jesus didn't always know exactly what to do and had to test the possibilities. That was quite an eye-opener to me!

Jesus had sent his disciples out without provision for their journey and then later with provision. Mrs. Eddy commented on that. "Why did he send forth his students first without, and then with, provision for their expenses? Doubtless to test the effect of both methods on mankind. That he preferred the latter is evident, since we have no hint of his changing this direction." (My. 215)

The question might then be: How could Jesus not know exactly what to do immediately? Why did he have to make a test? The clue to that, I believe, lies in this statement about him:

> ... all Christian Scientists deeply recognize the oneness of Jesus — that he stands alone in word and deed, the visible discoverer, founder, demonstrator, and great Teacher of Christianity, whose sandals none may unloose. (My. 338)

It's easy to accept that Jesus was the founder, demonstrator and Teacher of Christianity, but the discoverer too? How could that be? Reasoning it through, it's obvious that Jesus arrived on this scene with the understanding of the Christ, Truth. He was not called the discoverer of it. The Christ was his divine nature, and he knew it. He understood, as a boy of twelve, that he had to be about his Father's business, and he grew in that understanding.

But Jesus had to discover how to teach and demonstrate the Christ, Truth, in ways that could be lived and applied. That discovery was termed Christianity. It was an outcome of the Christ. If we accept that true Christianity is actually a *do,* not a *say* (as one I know likes to remark), then it's easy to see why it had to be discovered.

Testing mankind as he did was simply part of Jesus' discovery of Christianity. He had to know how it should be enacted. What a comfort that is to all of us! It's just so kind. Surely, we're even allowed to do the same as we make progress on our life journey.

Jesus always hit home runs (he hit it out of the park), but he still walked the sides and touched each point, each base. He gave the example for others to follow, but didn't do it for them.

> His mission was both individual and collective. He did life's work aright not only in justice to himself, but in mercy to mortals, — to show them how to do theirs, but not to do it for them nor to relieve them of a single responsibility. (S&H 18)

The Christian point of the city is illumined by stars, the Southern Cross, which show the sacrifice Jesus made and teaches us that we will have to do likewise. It's at that point we make sacrifices for others, and give up our false beliefs and wrong goals.

The south is the farthest base on the baseball diamond, on the compass, and in the sky. It's where we make the turnaround to go back up to the north. Again, the temptation may come to omit this point and run across the field ("let's avoid the sacrifice point"), but the divine law makes no such allowance.

This particular part of our journey will require us to recognize the general need of repentance and reformation, and will include noting the specific mistake and correcting it. It's useless to attempt to incorporate or simply graft the right onto the wrong in order to protect ourselves, or others, from the awful prospect of having to admit we were mistaken!

This era of political correctness would prefer we cut across the field and not admit to anything at all. Instead, we face those specifics and understand why it's necessary to recognize and correct even a small mistake, though it may mean we "lose face" in the process of doing so.

We want to get things right, but can't without admitting and correcting what is wrong. Mrs. Eddy said, "The knowledge of evil that brings on repentance is the most hopeful stage of mortal mentality." She went on to say the following:

> Even a mild mistake must be seen as a mistake, in order to be corrected; how much more, then, should one's sins be seen and repented of, before they can be reduced to their native nothingness!
> (Mis. 109)

As a dear friend of mine in England said, if we don't admit even to ourselves what is wrong, it becomes a guilty secret.

All along this path, and at every base we touch, we'll be required to constantly check our travel plans with the Bible, which is our map and guidebook, and to refer to the key to the map, which is *Science and Health*. Others' opinions can't enter in. This is the

Science of the Bible we're dealing with, and human opinions don't count.

Being born again, according to the Science of Christianity, is to come into a new sense of life—a spiritual, not a material one. It's so tempting to stand at the home plate of spiritual Life, Truth and Love, and declare we are already there.

Under the title, "The New Birth," the journey to this more exalted, spiritual sense of Life and Love is discussed, though the sweetness of our first awakening seems almost sufficient to us, and we exclaim, "... this is enough of heaven to come down to earth." (Mis.16)

However, we can't stand there on that new realization, but have to make the journey and run the bases by demonstrating Life, Truth, and Love. This is made clear in the preceding page describing the new birth.

> The new birth is not the work of a moment. It begins with moments, and goes on with years; moments of surrender to God, of childlike trust and joyful adoption of good; moments of self-abnegation, self-consecration, heaven-born hope, and spiritual love.

The journey will have its ups and downs, but it is so worth it. The "heaven-born hope" will keep us on the path and take us around the diamond. And just look at all the like-minded people we'll be traveling with, who contribute to the Christian Science periodicals! The correlation of these periodicals with the stars, going around the compass, is unmistakable. Mrs. Eddy called Jesus "this faithful sentinel" and said he "held uncomplaining guard over a world." (S&H 48, 49) She carefully named the four periodicals.

> I have given the name to all the Christian Science periodicals. The first was *The Christian Science Journal*, designed to put on record the divine Science of Truth; the second I entitled *Sentinel*, intended to hold guard over Truth, Life, and Love; the third, *Der Herold der Christian Science*, to proclaim the universal activity and availability of Truth; the next I named *Monitor*, to spread undivided the Science that operates unspent. The object of the *Monitor* is to injure no man, but to bless all mankind. (My 353)

Yes, we do have the light of the stars and good company as we travel, which help us maintain our joy, even when the going gets tough. We can always sing or hum along the way. Perhaps, the Willie Nelson song "On the Road Again" might be appropriate, as we begin on the highway that Earnest Eager saw on the front of the jigsaw puzzle.

GOLDEN ROAD RULES

When Earnest Eager left the baseball shop he went and sat under a tree to contemplate his next step. Yes, there he sat knowing he should start out on the highway and begin his journey, but once again something held him back. He had become so enthused by the truths that were being revealed to him, that he wanted to shout them out to everyone he met. But he knew that unrestrained zeal would be a hindrance. Finally, with quiet joy, Earnest set out to find the gold of prayer.

Almost immediately, he saw the sign, "Life's Highway," and noted there were always travelers on the rather dusty road. Some had no sense of purpose at all and just wandered aimlessly along, while many were taken up with daily duties, scurrying here and there. The aimless ones didn't seek the large or big picture. They didn't know they were on life's journey.

And for those immersed in daily details, there was also no opportunity to pause and consider the meaning of life's highway and its purpose. It was hard enough just keeping track of things in the ever-growing complexity of the modern world. Such travelers could easily lose an item or two on the road and never notice. The gold in plain sight could even be overlooked.

Other travelers might aim for the goal of success or fame, thinking that was the end, the big picture to life. But on gaining that goal, they have often become disillusioned. Then they either turned in a new direction or left life's highway altogether.

Earnest Eager kept the big picture in mind, as he overheard part of a conversation between businessmen passing him on the road. They were in a great hurry.

"I offered him a job, because he's a smart man with principles," said one man in a well-tailored suit. "Yup, I said he could take the high road, and we would take the low road, and we'd get 'em in the middle. But he didn't accept."

"That's strange," said one companion. "Hey, let's take a shortcut around the next corner."

The little group went out of range as they turned the corner. Earnest Eager knew the real goal in life wasn't a business goal but a goodness goal, so he kept that aim front and center, as he avoided the turnoffs from the highway. No cutting corners for him! He found out, as he walked along, there were two main road rules to obey, for they were posted prominently at every intersection to help travelers stay on the straight and narrow.

The first road rule was to love the Supreme Being, the intelligence of the universe, which was totally good, with all one's heart and the second was to love your neighbor as yourself. He wondered, as he passed each sign, if the first rule was like looking at the big or general picture, and the second was like the specifics of that picture. That thought intrigued him and also alerted him to watch for any other traveler, who might need help along the way.

One very good reason Earnest was glad he took the highway, instead of simply trying to land near the chapel, was because he could now see plainly that prayer without a journey was really prayer without a purpose. If he had skipped over this lesson, he would not have been totally prepared to find the gold of prayer. Even if he had found it, the true meaning or purpose of prayer would be lost on him. The pearls of wisdom and the diamond of hope revealed clearly what life was all about.

Life here on earth is a journey of great importance. The Guidebook told of a man who had walked among us. So many years ago, there was a spiritual, compassionate and divinely-appointed man who knew this road, who had traveled it and left the example of his path to be followed. If others would follow his travel route then, along the way, their burdens would be lifted. A whole new idea of life, divine Life, would be made plain. Some listened and followed, and some did not.

* * * * * * * * * * * * * * * *

There are road rules

Just as in taking up skydiving, there is preparation before taking the wheel of a car. At least there should be. A driver's license requires a few steps. After studying the manual, one has to pass a written test, then later a driving test. Many hours may be consumed in a training car with an instructor. Good preparation is a must for, at some point, a motorist will doubtless be faced with a situation that needs an immediate solution.

There are indeed two golden rules for the road. In giving his sense of the two great commandments in the law, Christ Jesus said that the Second Commandment to love our neighbor as ourselves was "like unto the first" which was to love God supremely. These go together as a pair, and if we desire to ascertain how much we really love God that is quite easy. "We should measure our love for God by our love for man." (*Miscellaneous Writings*, p. 12) That means we will not only watch out for ourselves, but for our fellow travelers as well.

On the road

"911. What is your emergency?"
"There's a sofa in the second lane of the 405 freeway going south, near the Westminster exit."
"Thank you. It has been reported already."

The operator was quick, polite and decisive, so hopefully not too many motorists after me would have to swerve around the obstacle in the darkening evening hours. Someone had evidently lost the sofa while moving. It was not unusual in California to see furniture piled high, sometimes loosely, on the back of a pickup truck, without covering of any kind. Obviously, someone's move was less than perfect, but the emergency road service could be counted on, and there was no doubt the offending item would soon be gone.

Prayer to God is often like calling on that road service. We are facing what appears to be a danger to others, and we call out to our heavenly Parent for help. "Please take care of this situation, that no one be harmed." Christ Jesus prayed that way for all those who would follow his pathway. He didn't ask to have them taken off the road, or their journey, but simply protected as they went along. "I pray not that thou shouldest take them out of the world, but that thou shouldest keep them from the evil." (John 17:15)

Prayer for our brother man does bring results, especially when the prayer is grounded on the understanding of God. In motoring terms, one needs to understand and have faith in the road service being provided.

Then there is the prayer for oneself in an emergency. A man once found himself in extreme circumstances when traveling a dark, narrow country lane at night. It was barely wide enough for one car. His passenger, a business acquaintance, sat silently watching the road, when suddenly headlights appeared out of nowhere, it seemed. They were headed straight for the man's vehicle. He told me there was no time to take action, and all he could do was to call out intuitively to God. Then everything changed!

A glance into the rear-view mirror startled the driver beyond all else. He saw tail-lights of a car behind him, receding and speeding into the distance and the dark. The car that had been on a direct collision course with his vehicle was now safely behind him, and on the same narrow road. The man's passenger began screaming and looked all around, even under his seat. There was no explaining what had happened, at least not in physical terms.

For years after that incident, the passenger sent the driver a card every Christmas. That wouldn't be too strange, one might imagine. However, the passenger was Jewish and the driver a man who had just awakened to the power of God. This was a man, who previously had little or no time for the Bible, religion, or for church going, and even less appreciation for the contribution or thinking of women in general. But having experienced an amazing, overnight healing of a crippling back condition, he was now an avid student of the Bible and of the book that helped open the healing power of the Bible to him, a book titled *Science and Health with Key to the Scriptures* by a New England woman, Mary Baker Eddy. His concept of God, the Bible, church, and women had all undergone a radical change! It was with that new perspective that he faced the oncoming car that dark night. And that made all the difference!

I didn't know about the incident until years later when the driver of that car and I were married. With our great love of Truth, this union or convergence of thought helped lead us into new paths of discovery together—paths that could be quite rocky. Glen would sometimes say to me jokingly, in the words of the country hit song, "I never promised you a rose garden." Nor does Mary Baker Eddy promise that in the chapter, "Prayer" where we find the following statement:

> Prayer means that we desire to walk and will walk in the light so far as we receive it, even though with bleeding footsteps, and that waiting patiently on the Lord, we will leave our real desires to be rewarded by Him. (S&H 13)

And the reader of this book isn't promised a flowery pathway either. But this has been found to be true that, as we follow the clues and travel the prayer path, our lives will never be the same again.

Help + a guidance system

When someone mentions triple A (AAA, the Automobile Association of America), what comes to mind? Usually, that means road help or emergency service to most people in the USA. And that is often the type of appeal made to God. This verse in Second Samuel is repeated in Psalm 18: "In my distress I called upon the Lord, and cried to my God: and he did hear my voice out of his temple, and my cry did enter into his ears." And there is also the plea, "Heal me, O Lord, and I shall be healed: save me and I shall be saved." (Jeremiah 17:14)

Paul advised the Romans to have faith in the help they were asking for: "... he that cometh to God must believe that he is, and that he is a rewarder of them that diligently seek him." (Hebrews 11:6) There is also this reassuring promise in Isaiah, "And it shall come to pass, that before they call, I will answer; and while they are yet speaking, I will hear." (Isaiah 65:24)

In other words, we can and should trust in God's constant help and care in any difficult situation, surely at least as much as we have faith in the roadside service we call upon.

However, no matter how good the help at hand is, and even if the spiritual answer comes immediately, there is more to being on life's highway with only the advantage of a divine emergency road service. As we abandon mere pleasure trips, think beyond running daily errands, and begin our spiritual life journey in earnest, it becomes obvious that divine Spirit, the divine Life which is God, is much more than our recourse in distress.

I have a friend who worked at triple A for 10 years, but usually didn't address roadside problems for motorists. That company provides maps, guidance, the best routes, times, mileage, car registration, and many other such details needed for a successful trip.

In the same way, prayer is so much more than a provision for reaching God quickly in times of need. Prayer to God moves us along on our travel path, showing us the best way to go and how to avoid the trouble spots. Prayer throws light on our destination and keeps us on track. God is truly our GPS or guidance system for the journey, and prayer accesses this system.

> And thine ears shall hear a word behind thee, saying, This is the way, walk ye in it, when ye turn to the right hand, and when ye turn to the left. (Isa.30:21)

An important point worth mentioning here is that we have to be traveling, or we wouldn't need a guidance system, as one cannot guide a stationary object.

Pausing to help

Let's return to the journey analogy for one more question. We may ask if we never delay our journey even to help another person in need. We have called in for help for another, asked that they be aided and blessed, and those prayers are answered, but is there a legitimate break in our journey? Yes, we may pause in our journey to aid another traveler. That's not an uncommon sight on a highway.

In one of his parables, Jesus tells of the Good Samaritan, who paused in his journey to Jerusalem, when he came across a man, who had been beaten and robbed. He even took the injured man on his own beast to an inn and used his own resources to help him. There were two other men, supposedly religious people, who were on the same road but evidently not on the same journey. They merely passed by the injured man. The Good Samaritan stopped to help.

It is the same with Christian Science treatment, when, with the permission of the individual, we use our own resources of spiritual enlightenment for someone, who has been beaten up by the world, in one way or another, and robbed of his sense of health and harmony. But the wonderful fact is revealed that those who have paused to minister to another's needs have lost no ground at all. Their good deed could never deprive them of their own progress. Instead it makes the path clearer than ever before.

The goal and the journey

Earnest Eager was right in his assessment that prayer without the journey was prayer without a purpose. Jesus told us to "Take up your cross and follow me." Luke's Gospel (9:23) even adds a word and says to take up the cross "daily, and follow me." Jesus expected us to be on the road of spiritual progress every day, if we were going to follow him.

He also counseled, "Seek ye first the kingdom of God, and his righteousness; and all these things shall be added unto you." (Matthew 6:33) All the provisions needed for our journey will be there, including health and healing. This is not an armchair endeavor of contemplating what Jesus did, but an active participation. It appears we have to not only walk the talk, but walk the thought.

Putting the journey first is being obedient to the divine command. Believing we are here on life's highway just to keep our bodies healthy, and going as long as possible, is to totally ignore our purpose on earth, the road we need to travel, and the progress we will have to make not only here but hereafter.

In the chapter, "Footsteps of Truth," on page 233, we find the following description of our goal:

> In the midst of imperfection, perfection is seen and acknowledged only by degrees. The ages must slowly work up to perfection. How long it must

be before we arrive at the demonstration of scientific being, no man knoweth, — not even "the Son but the Father;" but the false claim of error continues its delusions until the goal of goodness is assiduously earned and won.

That's the reason we are on life's highway, to achieve that "demonstration of scientific being" and to reach, "the goal of goodness."

The repair question and priorities

This discussion basically seems to boil down to two points of need—a guidance system for our journey and repair of our vehicle. Of the two, we find that our guidance system is the more important need. Simply repairing a car does not keep us on the right path and is not our main purpose. In other words, we don't own a car in order to repair it. That would be like saying a famous pianist is giving a concert in order to correct mistakes in his performance. His performance is the main issue. Mistakes can be corrected and technique improved along the way.

There's an interesting parallel between AAA and spiritual healing. That company is viewed as being almost exclusively for road service and repair, and many view the healing work in Christian Science as being mainly devoted to physical healing. Again, to emphasize this point, that would be rather like keeping our bodies, like cars, in good repair and safely garaged, hoping they will become antiques.

Opting for physical healing as our main goal is like simply trying to interest ourselves and others in a remedial agent or a garage for repairs. As important as that may be, there is a journey to be considered and that is our primary topic and aim.

No wonder Mary Baker Eddy had a strong answer for the question, "Is healing the sick the whole of Science." She replied on page 2 of her book, *Rudimental Divine Science*:

> Healing physical sickness is the smallest part of Christian Science. It is only the bugle-call to thought and action, in the higher range of infinite goodness. The emphatic purpose of Christian Science is the healing of sin; and this task, sometimes, may be harder than the cure of disease; because, while mortals love to sin, they do not love to be sick.

If you are wondering about physical healing and feel it's not as readily attainable as previously, there are a couple of good clues to follow as to why that might happen.

Physical healing is obviously lesser than the healing of sin, but it can perform a link to the higher mission. And just as in the explanation of the brotherhood of ideas, the lesser idea of God is a link to the higher, and the higher protects the lower. (S&H 518) By placing physical healing and the healing of sin out of order, and by making the lesser the greater, the link is lost. Furthermore, physical healing loses its protection and some of its effectiveness due to that mistake, and the journey is put into the shadows. A right order establishes a firm foundation for both. It protects physical healing and forwards the healing of sin. But another question emerges.

Why is the healing of sin the emphatic purpose of Christian Science? We can reason this out in a couple of ways, by seeing sin for what it is and then for what it does.

The reason sin is that which (in archery terms) misses the mark, is because the bulls-eye is doing God's will. Sin is the unwillingness to achieve that mark.

A friend wrote me that *Scofield's Reference Bible* defines sin as "The intrusion of self-will into the sphere of divine authority."

If the spiritual journey has the goal of goodness, then it is easy to see why sin, or self-will, which takes us off the mark, off the goodness highway, and off the path of spiritual progress, must be healed. This could explain why some turn off their spiritual GPS in order to follow their own desires and will.

Again, in the textbook of Christian Science is stated, on page 150 under the paragraph heading, "The main purpose:"

> ... but the mission of Christian Science now, as in the time of its earlier demonstration, is not primarily one of physical healing. Now, as then, signs and wonders are wrought in the metaphysical healing of physical disease; but these signs are only to demonstrate its divine origin, — to attest the reality of the higher mission of the Christ-power to take away the sins of the world.

The bugler plays reveille in the barracks to awaken the soldiers. Physical healing is a bugle call that awakens humanity to greater possibilities, to the battle with materiality and all it includes. Under the paragraph heading "Christian Warfare" in *Science and Health,* page 29, is the following: "Christians must take up arms against error at home and abroad. They must grapple with sin in themselves and in others, and continue this warfare until they have finished their course. If they keep the faith, they will have the crown of rejoicing."

Now, if the soldiers were awakened only to find there was no battle to be fought that day, eventually they may take to sleeping in. No need to answer that call if nothing of purpose awaits them. Similarly, physical healing becomes less relevant, and sadly less effective, without that higher purpose in mind. One could simply "sleep in late" and miss their hoped-for healing.

So, here we have at least two reasons why physical healing may be delayed, prolonged, or not even show up. It has been placed in the wrong position, superior to sin healing, or it is unrecognized as a wake-up call. The healing of sin, more than anything else will show how far we've traveled on life's highway.

Who is the Way-shower for our journey?

When planning a trip from Los Angeles to New York, we may consult many maps and services for our best route. We don't doubt that New York is there, or exists, even if we personally have never been there. When Jesus promised that the Kingdom of God is "at hand" he knew whereof he spoke. He had been there and was there. He knew, understood, true spiritual being and what it meant to be in that state of consciousness and to live it. He not only brought the Christ, Truth—that heavenly message from God to man telling of our real being—but he so lived the message that he became identified with it. However, the two are not truly synonymous as *Science and Health* points out. Christ is the divine message and Jesus is the messenger, the witness to the truth, who succeeded so well he was given the title Christ Jesus. Here was no ordinary messenger. There was a distinct reason for his success.

Human laws of procreation were set aside in the virgin birth, which enabled Jesus to represent both humanity and divinity. If his virgin birth seems far-fetched to some, let's remember that on a number of occasions in the Old Testament, women who were barren, or past child-bearing years, did indeed bear children. Those material laws had already been set aside to some degree. True, this was a giant step farther, but still in line with what had already been demonstrated. *Science and Health* explains it:

> Jesus is the name of the man who, more than all other men, has presented Christ, the true idea of God, healing the sick and the sinning and destroying the power of death. Jesus is the human man, and Christ is the divine idea; hence the duality of Jesus the Christ. (S&H 315)

We may ask if it is important to our life journey to understand Jesus and his mission. It is, because it tells of our destination and what we are aiming for. Jesus showed us the way to arrive at—to understand and experience—that spiritual selfhood which may appear dim, distant, or even non-existent to human thinking, though it truly exists right here and now.

This is the reason students of Christian Science follow Jesus' example and teaching, as it is integral to our life and our prayer path. This is not blind faith in an individual, but is similar to trustingly following a scout master up a steep hill, because he already has familiarity with what is at the top and knows well the pathway to reaching it. *Science and Health* on page 38 states, "Jesus mapped out the path for others." So, let us continue on our journey. The divine GPS or God Positioning System helps us. It curbs the wayward tendencies of misguided humanity to go off-road, off-track, over the cliff, and miss the mark. That's why we need a way-shower. Mrs. Eddy has this to say of Jesus and his accomplishment. (Ret. 26)

> Our great Way-shower, steadfast to the end in his obedience to God's laws, demonstrated for all time and peoples the supremacy of good over evil, and the superiority of Spirit over matter.

It's no wonder that multitudes have chosen to follow Jesus on life's highway!

Life's highway never ends

There is no end to life's highway because there is no end to life. It continues past earth's horizon and would be revealed as whole and complete if there were no earthly, material, limited views to interrupt it. A rainbow appears to have a beginning and an end. That appearance is false, and the "pot of gold" at the end of the rainbow is both fictional and inaccurate, for there is no end of the rainbow.

When flying from one Hawaiian island to another, Glen and I viewed a wonderful sight. A sudden rain shower gave way to sunlight, and a beautiful rainbow, whole and uninterrupted, appeared outside our plane window. It was a complete, multi-colored, unbroken circle simply floating in the sky. In the same way, as we rise higher spiritually, we'll find that life is unbroken, with no end at all.

That's what we are all doing on that dusty road. We're finding out what Life truly is, and prayer, put into action, is an integral part of that journey. This is such an important point to accept before considering prayer. Otherwise, we'd only use prayer to solve stationary everyday problems, when it has a much higher purpose than that.

Prayer is like turning on our guidance system for the journey. Prayer enables us to see the path more clearly. It reveals more of God, more of our true spiritual nature, and the possibility of demonstrating that nature. But lest we be impatient with ourselves or our journey, it's well to remember, "Imperfect mortals grasp the ultimate of spiritual perfection slowly; but to begin aright and to continue the strife of demonstrating the great problem of being, is doing much." (S&H 254)

We can help and encourage each other in many ways. We may even pray for our fellow travelers in the words of the hit country song, "Life's Highway," sung by Steve Wariner in the late 1980s. "May you never go astray on life's highway."

ORIENTATION TOUR

Earnest Eager was totally delighted to have finally made it to the prayer clue at the edge of the river. He could see now that this was not a church in the usual sense, not a gathering place, but a resting spot for the traveler. That was the service it provided. He entered with reverence and sat in silence for some time. Others found their way in and did likewise. It was a small, peaceful sanctuary.

The river glistened invitingly through the chapel's stained-glass windows, and Earnest felt beckoned by it but wouldn't hurry his time, as he was listening. He expected something, though he wasn't sure exactly what. He was not disappointed. All kinds of good ideas came flooding into Earnest's mind, and when he felt sufficiently filled, he got up and left on tiptoe so as not to disturb others.

It was only when Earnest looked around the chapel grounds more carefully that he noticed the sign-up sheet, displaying the instructions for those wanting to join the prayer excursion. This caused consternation among a few hopefuls, as they debated whether or not to sign up, It felt like quite a commitment. Nervously, some added their names.

The sign-up sheet warned that the trip was only for the sincere seeker for Truth, not for tourists. If tourist talk took over, the participants in that would be dropped off at the next stopping point. Questions should be of general interest and confined to the topic, so that all might be included in the answers. Every conclusion had to be checked for accuracy by consulting the Guide Book and the Key Book. Those reference materials could be accessed in the discovery room on board the boat. Anyone not willing to do that work would likewise be ushered off the boat.

In addition, those wanting to travel the prayer river should be *divested*, as much as possible, of the desire for fame and wealth, so they wouldn't be taking too much baggage and weigh the boat down. And the seekers should be *invested* in the kind care for others. Those special life vests would prove strong and useful, if they were to encounter turbulent, white water.

Finally, participants must first take the orientation tour to be held on a high rock near the chapel, unless they had traveled life's highway. The sign-up sheet was an agreement to the conditions of the journey. Earnest didn't have to think twice before adding his name, even for the orientation tour. He wanted to be sure he was pointed in the right direction. Then he waited patiently for everyone to assemble. He was full of joyful anticipation and shared that with the others who were waiting.

ORIENTATION TOUR

When Earnest's group was called to hike up to the top of the rock, he looked towards the highway and could see, way in the distance, Gerald Generic and Spencer Specific walking together, arms waving in animated conversation. Earnest smiled with happiness. They were on their way too!

※ ※ ※ ※ ※ ※ ※ ※ ※ ※ ※ ※ ※ ※ ※

Preliminary work

For those who have not traveled life's highway with the road rules, the two great commandments, in mind, or for those who doubt there is a guidance system available to them, this discussion will be necessary.

Though we'd like to set sail immediately to find our treasure, there's some preliminary work to be done. We first need to survey the landscape by climbing to a good vantage point. Though we are not feeling overwhelmed at this point, as did King David, his plaintive, poetic plea rings true for this expedition.

"Lead me to the rock that is higher than I"

A question immediately is asked why we couldn't just view the vast plain of human wisdom and knowledge that has been accumulated, which lies in front of us and is available at the tap of a finger on our iPad. Why do we have to expend so much energy climbing up higher? It's gently explained that such an accumulation is only that, a gathering of human observations and opinions. It's a flat plain with prairie dogs roaming around, arid patches of dry earth intermingled with sage brush. It's not really the hospitable learning landscape we seek, though it may include a billabong, a water hole, now and then to refresh us.

At this point, we may recall the experience of Colin Collector who landed in the cow pasture, and had to return to town in the company of various farm animals. A human accumulation of knowledge (gathering opinions together) or an accretion (building one opinion on top of another), isn't the orientation we need.

This is actually the first test of our willingness to explore the subject of prayer, and it's a very serious question. Are we willing to look higher than the human scene, or the human mind, for answers? Evidently not everyone is, for there are already a couple of departures, and so our group is now slightly smaller.

That request, that prayer from Psalm 61, to be led to a higher viewpoint or power, is perfect as the beginning of our search for the gold of prayer, and for a very good reason. It acknowledges there is a higher power—a wisdom greater than our own—to which we may turn.

This higher power or intelligence has been increasingly challenged of late. We're often told to "look within" for answers. The verbiage is rather constant and goes almost unnoticed. It may refer to "our inner child" or statements to the effect that there is an "artist in you," and a "healer in you," or even "the Christ in you." Now the point being made might be quite harmless, and could be just an attempt to indicate that we all have an innate ability. We all have access to the good we hope for, and that's quite true. The concept may be a general attempt to declare, in a roundabout way, that each of us has talents not even dreamed of, and they can be found and put to good use.

However, if those same statements imply that the divine *specifically* resides within the human, we have problems, and it's a detour to our journey. It's far safer to simply avoid that doubtful terminology because, "Christian Science eschews divine rights in human beings." (My. 303)

By allowing for that line of "in-you" reasoning, we may eventually even hear some proclaiming to be a co-creator with God, and the last step taken is to claim that they are God. At that point, "the rock that is higher than I" is no longer in sight, or remembered. There is no higher power to turn to other than our own being or intelligence.

That's pretty unnerving, and quite inaccurate too, of course, as so many have found through experiencing divine guidance and help. It all boils down to this statement from *Science and Health* on page 151. Referring to God as infinite Mind, this telling point is made. "Infinite Mind could not possibly create a remedy outside of itself, but erring, finite, human mind has an absolute need of something beyond itself for its redemption and healing."

Yes, that really sums it up, doesn't it, and is totally in accord with Biblical teaching both in the Old and New Testaments!

The "in-you" concept loses two very important aspects found in the Bible and explained through the Science of Christianity. First of all, the "in-you" teaching loses prayer. No need to pray to a higher power, but only look within yourself for answers. In order to keep our prayer quest on target, we hold onto the understanding of a higher power or intelligence to which we may pray.

Secondly, the "in-you" teaching loses reflection. All that there is of good exists in the Principle, God, not in His idea, spiritual man, who simply reflects that good as an image in a mirror would reflect the original. Man is made in God's image and likeness, we are told in the first chapter of Genesis. Man is not made to contain God, but to express God. The cause is not in the effect and cannot be, for the cause is greater than the effect and the greater cannot be in the lesser. It's an obviously straightforward concept on any level of life. This point is strongly made in *Science and Health* on page 467.

"Science reveals Spirit, Soul, as not in the body, and God as not in man but as reflected by man. The greater cannot be in the lesser. The belief that the greater can be in the lesser is an error that works ill. This is a leading point in the Science of Soul, that Principle is not in its idea."

Any goodness, wisdom, unselfishness, mercy or love we express is found to have originated in God, and is therefore reflected by and not contained within man seen humanly or divinely.

The common statement of a family resemblance, "Oh, I see your father in you," simply means a likeness to an individual. That father does not actually dwell within the child. So, we keep in mind the fact that we have the ability to reflect the divine power, not be it. The effect is not the cause though absolutely inseparable from it.

Science and Health describes God as the All-in-all, but again this means reflection not absorption. The following gives a clear picture of that. "God fashions all things, after His own likeness. Life is reflected in existence, Truth in truthfulness, God in goodness, which impart their own peace and permanence." (S&H 516)

The infinite All-in-all has no boundaries. If the divine All-in-all dwelt within its ideas, that which reflects it, God would become finite.

The belief that we are seeing God everywhere, and in everything, denies reflection. It virtually denies that God has an image and likeness. That concept is pantheism.

Mary Baker Eddy met straight on the challenge of pantheism, the "in-you" belief, in her small book *Christian Science versus Pantheism,* which was actually a message to her church in 1898. Interestingly, she ended that little volume with two pages on prayer for church and country. That seemed almost out of place to me at one time. Finally, I realized how better to handle pantheism than by ending with prayer, which goes beyond and outside of ourselves to a higher power. Prayer to God is the opposite of looking for God within us.

Looking for answers

The human tendency to hope for some kind of communication from departed loved ones is rather common. The damage occurs when hope is placed in a person to relay messages, information or comfort. Yes, it's often simply comfort the individual is hoping for when contacting psychics or mediums. Most of us have heard wonderful ideas or received inspirations without anyone else involved. They just came straight to our open and waiting consciousness from the divine Mind, God.

Mary Baker Eddy wrote a whole chapter in *Science and Health,* devoted to debunking any connection between Christian Science and spiritualism, which was very prevalent in her day. She explained the main point this way.

> In Christian Science there is never a retrograde step, never a return to positions outgrown. The so-called dead and living cannot commune together, for they are in separate states of existence, or consciousness. (S&H 74)

There is only one kind of such communication that is possible, and Mrs. Eddy explains this in that same chapter, "Christian Science versus Spiritualism."

> In Science, individual good derived from God, the infinite All-in-all, may flow from the departed to mortals; but evil is neither communicable nor scientific. (S&H 72)

The individual good that flows from the departed to us can only be found "in Science," within the understanding of the Science of Life. This is like saying we can only find answers to our math questions within the science of mathematics. Looking elsewhere doesn't truly work.

Those who practice physic readings or "channeling" could be most sincere in wanting to give others peace, comfort, and encouragement for the present or future. However, we're told that,

"Not personal intercommunion but divine law is the communicator of truth, health, and harmony to earth and humanity." (S&H 72)

An instance of this in my own life was recounted in my book, *Quiet Answers*. It took place a few years after my dearest Glen had passed, and I was faced with selling our car, affectionately termed Little Car, which was rather old at the time. This pulled at my heartstrings. Glen and I always believed in releasing whatever was unneeded, and I'd had very little trouble doing that previously. But this was different somehow. I prayed about it and still felt reluctant. One night, when I was chastising myself for that emotion, I said out loud these words, "Well, I know what Glen would say, if he were here!" Immediately I heard the mental response, "Keep it, honey. If it makes you feel better, keep it!"

This was rather startling to me for three reasons. First of all, I was sure Glen would tell me to get over it and get on with it. Secondly, I don't talk to myself in those endearing terms. Thirdly, I don't believe in spiritualism or that type of communication with those who have gone on.

But then I realized that divine Love was telling me what Glen would really say to me in this situation. I was basing my judgment on what we had done, or would do, together. Furthermore, if the situation had been reversed—if he had been here and feeling pulled about letting the car go, I would have said to him, "Keep it, honey. If it makes you feel better, keep it."

The next morning, I sold Little Car and was able to see it go off without any emotional wrench. What a comforting message that was, and how grateful I was for it! And there were other instances of metaphysical enlightenment that I considered to be "individual good derived from God," which have flowed to me from the departed. But I never figured these to be direct, personal communications, nor did I need an intermediary to bring them to me.

Though Jesus did not pass on in the traditional way, having ascended, he was still not on earth, on our plane of existence. After Jesus' ascension, John received a further communication containing more of Jesus' teaching. But this was not an audience or conversation with a personal Jesus. Rather was it the angel message that can come to us through the office of the Christ, Truth, which reveals divine truths to the human consciousness, to those who would wait with a listening ear, as John certainly did on Patmos.

There was no way to interfere with what Jesus sent to John. No human interpretation could change the message, and no stubborn human resistance could delay it. It was divine law that communicated Revelation, and John in turn, knowing it was Jesus' teaching, attributed the words and ideas to his great Teacher. At the right time, John heard the messages and recorded them.

Prayer enables us to listen to and receive the good we hope for, and no intermediary, religious or secular, is required. What a wonderful reassurance and a freedom that is!

The reality question

What is your reality? That's the question it often comes down to in mankind's efforts to find goodness in their lives. It's even suggested that we create our own reality. Unfortunately, that would make an individual responsible for all the problems surrounding him. But, it's the wrong question because it makes reality specific (to an individual) instead of generic (for everyone). It would be like saying one would be able to walk around in a bubble of sunshine, while it's raining on everyone else.

The thoughtful and humorous movie *The Truman Show* portrayed the opposite by having Jim Carey walk around under a cloud showering rain on him, while everyone else experienced sunshine. The cloud was manufactured by the unseen producers of a strange type of reality show, in which Jim was the unwitting star. Christ Jesus countered the concept of a specific reality for one person by telling us that God's goodness is impartial, "...he maketh his sun to rise on the evil and on the good, and sendeth rain on the just and on the unjust." (Matthew 5:45)

When we concentrate on our own specific reality, it's like being in that manufactured show, and no matter how wonderful it appears, it's not true goodness. Even more than that, it's a form of favoritism. The Calvinistic belief of predestination, in which some were chosen to be saved and others were not, promoted that view.

Reality has to be true for everyone, not only for selected people, just as math is true for everyone. Instead of concentrating on your or my reality, the question should be: What is the reality of life?

> As vapor melts before the sun, so evil would vanish before the reality of good. One must hide the other. How important, then, to choose good as the reality! (S&H 40)

While we don't create our own or any form of reality (we don't create 3x3=9), we do form our own experience by either disregarding reality, the law of good, or by coming into conformity with it. Coming into accord with the rules of math produces mathematical harmony in our lives. It's the same with rules or laws of goodness. "Hold thought steadfastly to the enduring, the good, and the true, and you will bring these into your experience proportionably to their occupancy of your thoughts." (S&H 261)

The reality of good is present for everyone, and each individual can experience it in proportion to the degree that it is welcomed into one's thinking.

Which one is prayer?

The high rock we have climbed is proving very useful. Furthermore, we now have the advantage of looking for clues regarding our journey, as we're becoming very eager to board our boat and travel the thought stream.

But just a little more patience is required while we become aware of another very important fact—one that Glen and I had to face at the beginning of our exploration. Something had happened to the gold of prayer.

It became apparent on our quest (more exciting to us than *Raiders of the Lost Ark*) that our gold had taken on various forms, so it no longer carried the same value. Our gold standard had changed. The term prayer had been so commonly used to refer to all kinds of spiritual thinking and speaking, from communing with God, to declarations of truth or even truthful arguments as in the practice of Christian Science, that the original meaning had been overlooked, even buried. This would be like looking at a wonderful landscape, such as the Grand Canyon, and calling everything "rock" even when it was a tree, a stream or an animal.

To use an active analogy, let's talk about traveling down that highway. Travel would be the generic term, but specifically one may run, jog, amble, crawl, hop, walk, skip, jump or drive down the road. How different each one is, and no one word, such as jog, can cover them all. And prayer had been used in this fashion. It seemed as though every good thought or right mental activity was termed *prayer* which was actually only one specific instance under the general heading of spiritual thinking. Paul told the Romans that to be "spiritually minded is life and peace."

There are so many facets of thinking and action included in being spiritually minded, such as contemplating, dwelling on, reviewing, or knowing the truth of God's creation. We could be declaring what is true, arguing for that truth, and just simply stating what is true. Yet, prayer has a distinct and specific meaning. It is a communication with God, and it is a desire, an asking.

For instance, *Westminster's Bible Dictionary* defines prayer as the communication of a child of God with its heavenly Parent. The practice of rendering prayer less precise by confusing it with other spiritual activities is challenged on the website Dictionary.com.

> Prayer in the Bible is converse with God; the intercourse of the soul with God, not "in contemplation or meditation, but in direct address to him."

Webster's Dictionary is very much in accord, stating that prayer may even be a single petition. It's definitely a communication with God, and that is how Jesus taught it, as a direct address, "Our Father."

For some time now, there has been popular endorsement for making positive affirmations, which are aimed at giving an individual the confidence to succeed in business or relationships. Central to the "make-your-own-reality" success movement, is the idea that what we think and claim can manifest what we desire. Popular books and movies have promoted this concept. It has literally swept over society and even into religion.

Some religions today make free use of what is termed "the prayer of affirmation," but this actually doesn't have a Biblical basis. Oh, there are indeed many statements of God's goodness and what He has done all throughout the Scriptures, but these usually fall into the category of praise declarations because, on their own, statements do not fit the prayer, or communication, definition. Declarations or strong statements of God's goodness and power may accompany prayer, the petition, as the reason given for why God would answer our prayer.

We could take a few verses from the Psalms of David as examples of this point. In Psalm 6, David asks God to hear him, stating it is to God (obviously not to man) to whom he will pray. It's also worthy of note that King David addresses God as his King: "Hearken unto the voice of my cry, my King, and my God: for unto thee will I pray."

Then he further states his faith in God's good nature. "For thou art not a God that hath pleasure in wickedness: neither shall evil dwell with thee."

Here again, in Psalm 69, the Psalmist is asking God to hear him based on his trust in God's love and care. "Hear me, O Lord; for thy lovingkindness is good: turn unto me according to the multitude of thy tender mercies."

Yes, many strong declarations can be found within prayer, but they do not stand alone as prayer. How wonderful to talk with our heavenly Parent and hear messages of good that are meant just for us! No statement about God, as important as it may be, could ever take the place of communicating with our Father-Mother, God.

On holy ground

Our spiritual landscape is now coming more fully into view, and the distinct or specific features of it are more apparent. Rather than terming all holy attitudes or statements as prayer, we can see that the whole landscape is spiritual, and therefore holy.

Perhaps, the tendency to term all spiritual vocabulary and thinking as prayer, arose from the need to show holiness. If we refer to arguing a case that might simply pertain to a court of law. Declarations or statements of fact might be made to a notary public. Knowing the truth of our origin could be part of an anthropology class. How to show all these activities to be holy might be a problem.

If we determine that the context in which we are speaking is a divine one, and the facts of being, or arguments of truth, all pertain to God and His children, then we are already on holy ground. There is no need to cover these terms with the blanket of prayer to protect them or maintain their sacredness. We are allowed and, even more, we are mandated in this quest to be accurate.

With the concept of accuracy foremost in our thinking, and the fact that prayer means we are communicating or talking with God, we're ready to board our boat for the prayer expedition and search.

We have all the resources we need at our fingertips, but the most important one of all is to possess the right spirit for the journey.

ALL ABOARD!

Earnest Eager was thrilled to finally be boarding the boat for the prayer trip. Other passengers were also exclaiming over the privilege of being included on the search. Realizing it wouldn't matter where he sat, Earnest found a chair on the deck, where he could view those still boarding, as well as the water traffic that was passing by on the river.

Glancing at the group walking across the gangplank, he was sorry to see that not everyone had been willing to sign up and agree to the conditions of the expedition. He realized that many people hope for a joyride through life like tandem skydiving, strapped to someone or something for security. The process of learning life's solo journey was quite another matter. Evidently, some would-be travelers were not really committed to being seekers of Truth. Earnest sighed and turned his attention to the river.

He couldn't help smiling as he saw speeding boats, going in opposite directions, filled with some skydivers he knew, searching for the gold of prayer. "This is going to be quite a journey," Earnest told himself and, as it turned out, he was quite right!

* * * * * * * * * * * * * * *

How well I recall, a time or two in my youth, when our family saw people off at Sydney Quay, as they took passenger ships bound for faraway places such as America. Our imaginations followed them across the Pacific Ocean to ports with landmarks like the Golden Gate Bridge.

Streamers would be thrown down to us by our friends standing at the rails, and those multi-colored strands connected land and sea until the ship, sounding its horn, sailed beyond the length of the streamers. It was a fond farewell.

When I was in my mid-teens, our family took off on our own adventure, but this being by air there were no streamers. However, my classmates at Sydney Girls' High School told me they took a sheet to the lower grounds, so they could wave goodbye as our plane, bound for America, flew overhead. It was lovely to hear about, even though we didn't see it.

Some of our experiences, after leaving Australia, are recounted by my dad, John H. Wyndham, in his book *The Ultimate Freedom*. After living in different countries and states, during both good and trying times, I have an observation to make. No trip, or journey, no human voyage, has ever come even close to the divine adventure gained through the study and application of Christian Science. I'm sure many readers have also found this to be true.

Due to that fact, I do hope that you have felt enriched by this exploration, and will join in the next installment.

As we say farewell for now to Earnest Eager and his boatload of seekers, we can expect to catch up with them all on *The Golden Prayer Search*.

Until then, streamers of good wishes are thrown out to you, dear reader. May your spiritual journey be full of joy!

For ordering and author information
please visit the Mountaintop website:
www.MountaintopPublishing.com

www.ingramcontent.com/pod-product-compliance
Lightning Source LLC
Chambersburg PA
CBHW070641050426
42451CB00008B/256